ADDICTED TO WAR

Why the U.S. Can't Kick Militarism

an illustrated exposé
by Joel Andreas

Endorsements for *Addicted to War*:

"*Addicted to War* is must reading for all Americans who are concerned with understanding the true nature of U.S. foreign policy and how it affects us here at home."
—**Martin Sheen**
Actor

"*Addicted to War* is a rare gift to the American people. It should be read by every person who cares about the human condition. This book reveals truths that all Americans need to understand if we are ever to experience peace and justice for all the people of the earth."
—**Father Roy Bourgeois***
Founder of School of the Americas Watch

"This book analyzes why men are addicted to fighting and killing—an addiction that could, in this the nuclear age, destroy all life on earth, creating the final epidemic of the human race."
—**Helen Caldicott**
Pediatrician and author of Missile Envy

"*Addicted to War* graphically exposes the U.S. propensity to make war and should be required reading in every school in the country, including military schools!"
—**Ann Wright***
Retired U.S. Army Reserve Colonel who resigned in 2003 to oppose the Iraq war

"As we're goose-stepping our way into the new millennium, Addicted to War provides us with an opportunity to see ourselves as others see us."
—**Kris Kristofferson***
Singer/songwriter

"Political comics at its best. Bitterly amusing, lively, and richly informative. For people of all ages who want to understand the link between U.S. militarism, foreign policy, and corporate greed at home and abroad."
—**Michael Parenti**
Author of *History as Mystery* and *To Kill a Nation*

"*Addicted to War* makes one point perfectly clear: We can bomb the world to pieces, but we can't bomb it into peace!"
—**Michael Franti**
Musician, Spearhead

"The enormous criminal impact of U.S. militarism on the people of the world and the U.S. is hard to grasp. This book makes it easier to understand. Now we must act."
—**Ramsey Clark***
Former U.S. Attorney General

"*Addicted to War* should be required reading for every student in America. I encourage educators to use it to help students understand the consequences of U.S. militarism for people here and around the world."
—**Rev. J. M. Lawson**
Colleague of Martin Luther King, Jr. from 1957–68

"Our young people will learn more about the cult of militarism in this short and accurate book by Joel Andreas than they might learn in their first twelve years of schooling."
—**Blase Bonpane***
Director of Office of the Americas

"*Addicted to War* is the BEST primer on why the US goes to war and the devastating consequences of our addiction. It should be in high schools, colleges, churches, libraries and community centers. It should be gifted to graduates and passed on to relatives and colleagues. Why? Because there's no other book about such a profound—and depressing—topic as war that is so much fun to read!"
—**Medea Benjamin**
Cofounder of CODEPINK and author of *Drone Warfare: Killing by Remote Control*

"Read this book!"
—**Cindy Sheehan**
Founding member of Gold Star Families for Peace

"The idiocy of war is apparent. What is amazing is that no matter the tracts, essays and books telling us this through the ages, we resist that truth. Hopefully this political comic by Joel Andreas can pierce the tough hide of man's mind and heart."
—**Edward Asner***
Actor

"The U.S. arrogantly plunders resources and cultures to support its American Way of Life. *Addicted to War* illustrates why the U.S. is necessarily dependent upon war to feed its shameful consumption patterns."
—**S. Brian Willson***
Vietnam veteran, anti-war activist

"For those who have created a wall in their mind to resist questioning what the powers-that-be have taught them, this book may be the right battering ram."
—**William Blum**
Author of *Killing Hope* and *Rogue State*

"Lots of people wonder why the U.S. is always going to war one place or another around the world. I tell them to read Addicted to War."
—**Cynthia McKinney**
Former Congresswoman from Georgia

"This book has educated more people than the past decade's worth of the New York Times and done so with more humor, erudition and wisdom. This is a book to buy in bulk and give to everyone you know. The tide is starting to turn."
—**David Swanson**
Author of *War Is a Lie*

"This is the most important comic book ever written. To be a true patriot (in the American revolutionary sense) is to understand the cruelty of U.S. foreign policy. Read this book and pass it on to as many people as you can."
—**Woody Harrelson**
Actor

"I've come to the conclusion that if we don't change from a value system based on love of money and power to one based on love of compassion and generosity we will be extinct this century. We need a brief earthquake to wake up humanity. *Addicted to War* is such an earthquake."
—**Patch Adams, M.D.**
Founder of Gesundheit Institute, Vietnam War-era conscientious objector

"How can we wean ourselves from our dismal addiction to war? This book is a fine starting point. Reading it will help people get on the road to recovery."
—**Kathy Kelly**
Founder of Voices in the Wilderness

"War may be the 'health of the state,' as Randolph Bourne warned when a pacifist population was being driven to World War I by hysterical propaganda, but it is the curse of the people—the attackers and the victims. With spare and acid clarity, these snapshots of the real world brilliantly tell us why and how we must rid ourselves of this curse, quickly, or else descend into barbarism and destruction."
—**Noam Chomsky**
Author and Professor Emeritus, MIT

"*Addicted to War* should be assigned reading in U.S. schools because it tells the true history of this nation's culture of war. Many young students will think twice before considering enlistment in the military. How different things might have been had my son had a chance to read it. However, it's not too late for many thousands of young Americans."
—**Fernando Suarez del Solar**
Father of Jesús Suarez del Solar, who died fighting in Iraq

*Served in the U.S. military

Frank Dorrel
P.O. Box 3261
Culver City, CA 90231-3261
310-838-8131
fdorrel@addictedtowar.com
www.addictedtowar.com

AK Press
674-A 23rd Street
Oakland, CA 94612-1163
(510) 208-1700
akpress@akpress.org
www.akpress.org

JOEL ANDREAS began following his parents to demonstrations against the Vietnam War while in elementary school in Detroit. He has been a political activist ever since, working to promote racial equality and workers' rights inside the United States and to stop U.S. military intervention abroad. After working as an automobile assembler, a printer, and a civil engineering drafter, he completed a doctoral degree in sociology at the University of California in Los Angeles, studying the aftermath of the 1949 Chinese Revolution. He now teaches at Johns Hopkins University in Baltimore. *Addicted to War* is Joel's third illustrated exposé. He wrote and drew *The Incredible Rocky*, an unauthorized biography of the Rockefeller family (which sold nearly 100,000 copies) while a student at Berkeley High School in California. He also wrote another comic book, *Made with Pure Rocky Mountain Scab Labor*, to support a strike by Coors brewery workers.

<u>Photograph and Drawing Credits</u>

Page 3: Artist unknown | Page 4, upper: J.E. Taylor, J. Karst | Page 4, lower: New York Historical Society | Page 6: U.S. Army Signal Corps | Page 7, upper: Mayol |Page 7, middle: U.S. National Archives | Page 7, lower: W.A. Rogers | Page 9, upper: Karen Glynn & Eddie Becker Archive | Page 9, lower: U.S. Government (Forward March) | Page 11: Yosuke Yamahata | Page 13: U.S. Department of Defense | Page 14: Ngo Vinh Long collection | Page 15, upper and lower: U.S. Dept. of Defense | Page 20: Mary Martin | Page 25, upper and lower left: Commission of Inquiry for the International War Crimes Tribunal | Page 25, right: *New York Times* | Page 31: Amir Shah, Associated Press | Page 34: Muhammed Muheisen, Associated Press | Page 35: U.S. Dept. of Defense, courtesy of Wikileaks | Page 37: Noor Behram | Page 53: McCormick Research Center | Page 54: John Schreiber | Page 56: Family of Tomas Young | Page 62: Harvey Richards, War Resisters League | Page 63, upper: Brian Shannon | Page 63, lower: John Gray | Page 65, upper: Bernard Edelman | Page 65, lower: Flax Hermes | Page 66: Steven Gross | Page 67, upper: Deirdre Griswold, Int'l Action Center | Page 67, lower: Bill Hackwell

<u>To order more copies:</u>
To order more copies of *Addicted to War*, contact either Frank Dorrel or AK Press. Please ask about bulk rates! *Addicted to War* is also available through your local bookstore and online book dealers. To receive an AK Press catalog, please write or visit the AK Press website (above).

<u>*Addicted to War* in other languages:</u>
To order a Spanish edition of *Addicted to War* in the United States, contact Frank Dorrel or AK Press. The book has also been published in Belgium, the Czech Republic, Denmark, Finland, Germany, Hungary, India, Indonesia, Italy, Japan, South Korea, Spain, and Thailand. To find out how to obtain copies of these translated editions, see: www.addictedtowar.com.

Table of Contents

Sources are listed starting on page 72 and are referenced throughout the book with circled numbers. All statements in "quotation marks" are actual quotes.

Author's Preface to the 2015 Edition

I wrote the first edition of *Addicted to War* after the first U.S. war against Iraq in 1991. Ten years later, following the U.S. invasion of Afghanistan, Frank Dorrel convinced me to update the book. The ink had barely dried on the new 2002 edition when the invasion of Iraq compelled me to revise the book again. That edition came out in early 2004. The decade since then has seen an endless binge of war-making and unfortunately I can't escape from updating the book again. As we're set to publish this edition, the Obama Administration continues to wage wars in Afghanistan, Iraq, and Syria while pioneering a new type of warfare in which the killing is done by remote control. With militarized drones patrolling the world's skies, we may be entering an era of warfare without beginning or end and without defined battlefields.

I wrote *Addicted to War* to introduce readers to the long history of U.S. foreign wars so that they might better understand the reasons our country wages war today. The book chronicles over two centuries of warfare, starting with the Indian wars. During this time, America's machinery of war has grown into a behemoth that dominates our economy and society and extends around the globe. The costs of our country's addiction to war are felt acutely at home. Soldiers and their families are paying the heaviest price, but everyone is affected. Massive military spending is contributing to huge government deficits and causing sharp cuts in domestic programs, including education, health care, housing, public transport, and environmental protection. At the same time, combatting terrorism is being used as an excuse to step up police surveillance and erode our civil liberties. I hope this book will help spur reflection and debate about militarism and encourage creative action to break this addiction.

It's impossible to thank here all of the people who have contributed to the creation of this book. Instead, I will mention only three: My mother, Carol Andreas, who introduced me to anti-war activities; my father, Carl Andreas, who first encouraged me to write the book; and Frank Dorrel, whose tireless promotion made each new edition possible.

Joel Andreas, January 2015

Publisher's Note

I first read *Addicted to War* in 2000. That was the original 1991 edition. I thought it was the best book I had ever read, revealing the true history of U.S. militarism. I located the author/illustrator, Joel Andreas, and convinced him to update the book. In 2002, I published a new edition with the help of AK Press. The response has been tremendous. Since then, close to 240,000 copies—in English and Spanish—have been distributed in the U.S. and Canada. We are now proud that the updated 2015 edition is available.

Addicted to War is being used as a textbook by many high school teachers and college professors. Peace organizations are selling the books at anti-war rallies, teach-ins and smaller events. It is showing up in churches and public libraries and more and more bookstores are carrying it. Individuals are ordering multiple copies to give to friends, co-workers and relatives. I have received thousands of calls, email messages and letters from people telling me how much they love and appreciate this book!

I want to thank Joel Andreas for giving us a powerful educational tool that reveals the sad and painful truth. Thanks to Yumi Kikuchi and Gen Morita for their support and for making the Japanese edition possible. Thanks to the Veterans for Peace and to the other anti-war organizations listed at the back of the book for using it to help raise awareness. We are honored that some of America's most courageous peace educators and activists have endorsed the book. Thanks to Blase Bonpane and KPFK 90.7 FM Radio in Los Angeles for teaching me the truth about US foreign policy. Thanks to AK Press for co-publishing *ATW* with me. And thanks to my friends, to my family and to S. Brian Willson for supporting this project from the beginning.

Finally, I want to thank you the reader for your concern about the issues addressed in this book. I encourage you to use it to help bring about a change of consciousness in this country. Please consider taking a copy to a teacher who might use it in class. Take a copy to your church, synagogue or mosque. Send one to your congressperson, city council member, or someone in the media. Show it to friends and family. And also encourage them to listen to or watch *Democracy Now,* hosted by Amy Goodman. It's up to each of us to do our part. Education is the key. We can make a difference, all of us together. People around the world are counting on us to end our country's addiction to war.

Frank Dorrel, January 2015

Our story begins on a Friday afternoon.

Yeow! Look at all the **money** the government took out of my **paycheck!**

Later that evening:

Mom – they want you to help at a **bake sale** so my school can buy **toilet paper.**

First no **books** and now no **toilet paper!** Do they have **anything** at your school?

At the next school board meeting:

I'm **sorry,** the local tax base is declining and we get **very little help** from the federal government. There's just **no money!**

What do they **do** with all the **taxes** I pay?

A huge part of the money the **IRS** takes out of our paychecks goes to support the military. **Military spending** adds up to **more than half** of the Federal Government's annual discretionary spending.

Federal Discretionary Budget
fiscal year 2014

① Including **education** spending, **6%**

Military Spending 55%

Everything else 45%

No wonder there's **no** toilet paper!

The United States maintains the largest and **most powerful military in history**. U.S. warships dominate the oceans, its missiles and bombers can strike targets on every continent, and hundreds of thousands of U.S. troops are stationed overseas. Every few years the U.S. sends soldiers, warships and warplanes to **fight in distant countries**. Many countries go to war, but the U.S. is **unique** in both the **size and power** of its military and its **propensity to use it**.

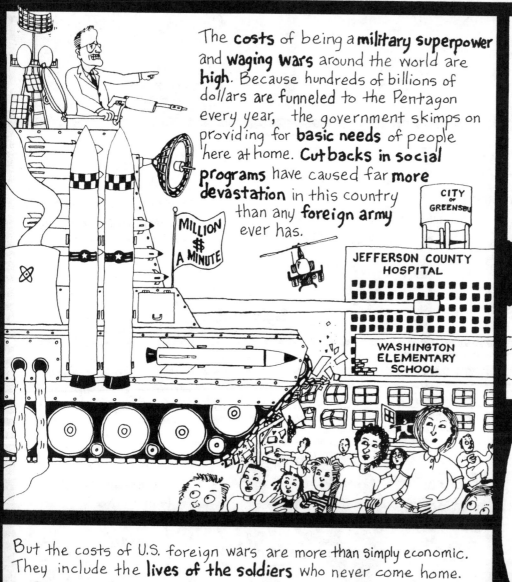

The **costs** of being a **military superpower** and **waging wars** around the world are **high**. Because hundreds of billions of dollars are funneled to the Pentagon every year, the government skimps on providing for **basic needs** of people here at home. **Cutbacks in social programs** have caused far **more devastation** in this country than any **foreign army** ever has.

MILLION $ A MINUTE

CITY OF GREENSBU

JEFFERSON COUNTY HOSPITAL

WASHINGTON ELEMENTARY SCHOOL

Foreign wars also bring **bloody retaliation** against the U.S. — such as the **terrorist attacks** that took the lives of thousands of people at the **Pentagon** and the **World Trade Center**.

Despite the high costs in **money and lives**, the government seems determined to keep going to war, **putting us all in harm's way!**

But the costs of U.S. foreign wars are more than simply economic. They include the **lives of the soldiers** who never come home.

But why is the United States always **getting into wars**?

Good question!

Two centuries ago, the United States was a collection of **thirteen small colonies** on the Atlantic coast of North America. Today it **dominates the globe** in a way that even the most powerful of past empires could not have imagined.

The path to **world power** has **not** been **peaceful**

I'll have to read up on this...

Chapter 1
"Manifest Destiny"

The **American revolutionaries** who rose up against **King George** in 1776 spoke eloquently about the **right of every nation to determine its own destiny.**

"When in the course of human events it becomes necessary for one people to **dissolve** the political bands which have connected them with another, and assume, among the **Powers of the earth**, the separate and equal station to which the Laws of Nature and of Nature's God **entitle them...**"

Thomas Jefferson, from the <u>Declaration of Independence</u>, 1776

Unfortunately, after they won the right to determine **their own destiny** they thought they should determine **everyone else's** too!

The leaders of the **newly independent colonies** believed that they were **preordained** to rule all of North America. This was so obvious to them that they called it **"Manifest Destiny."**

"We must march from **ocean to ocean**. ...It is the destiny of the **white race**."

Representative Giles of Maryland

This "manifest destiny" soon led to genocidal wars against the **Native American peoples.** The U.S. Army ruthlessly **seized** their land, driving them west and slaughtering those who resisted.

During the century that followed the American Revolution, the Native American peoples were defeated one by one, their lands were taken, and they were confined to **reservations.** The number of dead has never been counted. But the tragedy did not end with the dead. The Native peoples' **way of life** was devastated. ③

"I can still see the butchered women and children lying heaped and scattered all along the crooked gulch as plain as when I saw them with eyes still young. And I can see that something else died there in the bloody mud, and was buried in the blizzard. A **people's dream** died there. It was a beautiful dream ...the nation's hoop is **broken and scattered.**" ④

Black Elk, spiritual leader of the Lakota people and survivor of the Wounded Knee massacre in South Dakota

By 1848 the United States had seized **nearly half of Mexico's territory.**

United States

Wyoming

Nevada

California

Utah

Colorado

Kansas

Arizona

New Mexico

Oklahoma

Texas

Territory Seized from Mexico

Mexico

In Congress the war against Mexico was justified with speeches about the glory of expanding "Anglo-Saxon democracy," but in truth it was the Southern slave owners' thirst for land and the lure of Western gold that inspired these speeches. ⑤

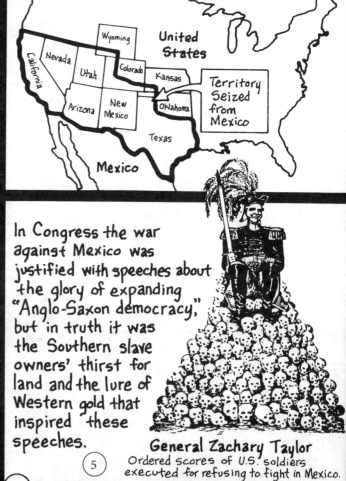

General Zachary Taylor Ordered scores of U.S. soldiers executed for refusing to fight in Mexico.

With their domain now stretching from **coast to coast** the "Manifest Destiny" crowd began to dream of an **overseas empire**. Economic factors drove these ambitions. Col. Charles Denby, a railroad magnate and an ardent **expansionist**, argued: ⑥

"Our condition at home is **forcing** us to commercial expansion... Day by day, **production is exceeding home consumption**... We are after markets, the greatest **markets** in the world."

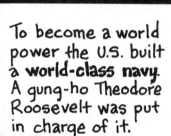

Calls for **empire** were echoing through the halls of Washington.

"I firmly believe that when any territory outside the **present territorial limits** of the United States becomes necessary for our defense or essential for our commercial development, we ought to **lose no time** in acquiring it."

Senator Orville Platt of Connecticut, 1894 ⑦

To become a world power the U.S. built a **world-class navy**. A gung-ho Theodore Roosevelt was put in charge of it. ⑧

"I should **welcome** almost **any war**, for I think this country **needs one**."

T. Roosevelt, 1897

He didn't have **long** to wait.

The next year, taking a fancy to several Spanish colonies, including **Cuba and the Philippines**, the U.S. declared war on Spain. **Rebel armies** were already fighting for **independence** in both countries and Spain was on the verge of defeat. Washington declared that it was on the rebels' side and Spain quickly capitulated. But the U.S. soon made it clear that it had **no intention of leaving**. ⑨

"The Philippines are **ours forever**... and just beyond the Philippines are China's illimitable markets... the Pacific is **our ocean**."

Senator Albert Beveridge of Indiana, 1900

And for the Senator, the Pacific was **only the beginning**:

"The power that rules the Pacific is the power that **rules the world**... That power is and will forever be the American Republic."

⑩

Elaborate **racist theories** were invented to **justify colonialism** and these theories were adopted enthusiastically in Washington. (11)

"We are the **ruling race of the world.** ...We will not renounce our part in the mission of our race, **trustee, under God** of the civilization of the world. ...He has marked us as **his chosen people**... He has made us **adept in government** that we may administer government among **savage and senile peoples.**"

Senator Albert Beveridge, again

But the Filipinos didn't share the views of Senator Beveridge and his buddies.

They fought the new invaders just as they had fought the Spanish. The U.S. subjugated the Philippines with brute force.
U.S. soldiers were ordered to " **Burn all and kill all,** " and they did. By the time the Filipinos were defeated, **600,000 had died.** (12)

U.S. soldiers stand on the bones of Filipinos who died in the war

The **Philippines, Puerto Rico,** and **Guam** were made into **U.S. colonies** in 1898. Cuba was formally given its independence, but along with it the Cubans were given the Platt Amendment, which stipulated that the **U.S. Navy** would operate a base in Cuba **forever,** that the U.S. Marines would **intervene at will,** and that Washington would determine Cuba's foreign and financial policies. (13)

Now, don't say I never gave you anything.

Independence

Platt Amendment

During the same period, the U.S. **overthrew Hawaii's Queen Liliuokalani** and transformed these unspoiled Pacific islands into a **U.S. Navy base** surrounded by Dole and Del Monte plantations. In 1903, after Theodore Roosevelt became president, he sent **gunboats** to secure **Panama's** separation from Colombia. The Colombian government had refused Roosevelt's terms for building **a canal**. (14)

If they won't sell, I'll just take it!

Then Uncle Sam began sending his Marines **everywhere**

The Marines went to China, Russia, North Africa, Mexico, Central America, and the Caribbean. (15)

♫ From the Halls of Montezuma to the shores of Tripoli... ♫

Troops march in Siberia during the U.S. invasion of Russia, 1918

Between 1898 and 1934, the Marines invaded Cuba 4 times, Nicaragua 5 times, Honduras 7 times, the Dominican Republic 4 times, Haiti twice, Guatemala once, Panama twice, Mexico 3 times, and Colombia 4 times! (16)

In many countries, the Marines stayed on as an **occupying army,** sometimes for decades. When the Marines finally went home, they typically left the countries they had occupied in the hands of a **friendly dictator,** armed to the teeth to suppress his own people.

Behind the Marines came **legions of** U.S. business executives ready not only to sell their goods but also to set up **plantations**, drill **oil wells**, and stake out **mining claims**. The Marines returned when called upon to enforce **slave-like working conditions** and put down **strikes, protests,** and **rebellions**.

Standard Oil   United Fruit   Domino Sugar   Anaconda Copper

(17)

"[I accept responsibility for] active intervention to secure for **our capitalists** opportunity for **profitable investments**."

(18)

President William Howard Taft, 1910

A reporter described what took place after U.S. troops landed in **Haiti in 1915** to put down a **peasant rebellion**:

American marines opened fire with machine guns from airplanes on defenseless Haitian villages, killing men, women and children in the open market places for sport.

(19)   (20)   50,000 Haitians were killed.

General Smedley Butler was one of the most celebrated leaders of these **Marine expeditions**. After he retired, he reconsidered his career, describing it as follows:

"I spent 33 years and 4 months in active **military service**... And during that period I spent most of my time as a **high-class muscle man for Big Business**, for Wall Street and the bankers. In short, I was a racketeer, a **gangster for capitalism**."

(21)

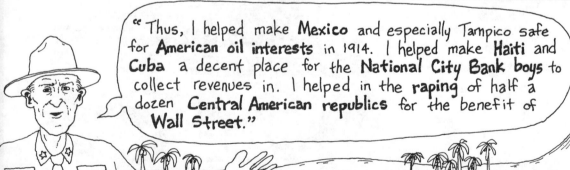

"Thus, I helped make **Mexico** and especially Tampico safe for **American oil interests** in 1914. I helped make **Haiti** and **Cuba** a decent place for the **National City Bank boys** to collect revenues in. I helped in the **raping** of half a dozen **Central American republics** for the benefit of **Wall Street**."

"I helped **purify Nicaragua** for the international banking house of Brown Brothers in 1902-1912. I brought light to the **Dominican Republic** for **American** sugar interests in 1916. I helped make **Honduras** right for **American fruit** companies in 1903. In **China** in 1927, I helped see to it that **Standard Oil** went on its way unmolested."

U.S. Marine officer with the head of Silvino Herrera, one of the leaders of Augusto Sandino's rebel army, Nicaragua, 1930

World War I was a horrific battle among the **European colonial powers** over how to **divide up the world**. When President Woodrow Wilson decided to **enter the fray**, he told the American people that he was sending troops to Europe to "**make the world safe for democracy**."

But what Wilson was **really after** was what he considered to be the United States' **fair share of the spoils.**

Wilson's ambassador to England said rather forthrightly that the U.S. would declare war on Germany because it was...

(22)

"...the **only way** of maintaining our present **pre-eminent trade status.**"

Ambassador W.H. Page, 1917

For this, **130,274** U.S. soldiers were **sent to their deaths.** (23)

"Our boys were sent off to die with **beautiful ideals** painted in front of them. No one told them that **dollars and cents** were the real reason they were marching off to **kill and die.**"

General Smedley Butler, 1934

World War I was **supposed** to be the "**war to end all wars.**"

It wasn't.

During **World War II**, millions of young Americans signed up to fight **German fascism** and **Japanese imperialism**. But the goals of the strategic planners in Washington were far **less admirable.**

They had **imperial ambitions** of their own.

In October 1940, as German and Japanese troops were **marching in Europe and Asia**, a group of **prominent government officials, business executives, and bankers** was convened by the U.S. State Department and the Council on Foreign Relations to discuss U.S. strategy. They were concerned with maintaining an **Anglo-American "sphere of influence"** that included the British Empire, the Far East, and the Western hemisphere. They concluded that the country had to **prepare for war** and come up with...

"... an integrated policy to achieve **military and economic supremacy** for the United States."

Yes! Yes! Yes!

(24)

Of course, they didn't say this **publicly,**

If war aims are stated which seem to be concerned solely with Anglo-American imperialism, they will offer little to people in the rest of the world... The interests of other peoples should be stressed... This would have a better propaganda effect. (25)

From a private memorandum between the Council on Foreign Relations and the State Department, 1941

A horrendous war was concluded with a horrendous event: **200,000 people were killed** instantaneously when the U.S. dropped **nuclear bombs** first on **Hiroshima** and then on **Nagasaki**. Tens of thousands more died later from radiation poisoning.

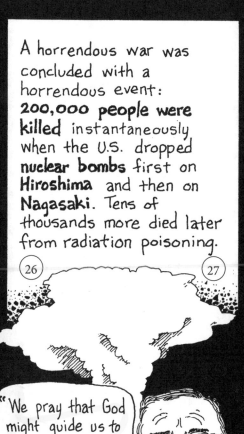

"We pray that God might guide us to use [the Bomb] in **His** ways and for **His** purposes."

President Harry Truman, 1945

The defeat of Japan had already been assured **before** the bombs were dropped. Their main purpose was to **demonstrate** to the world the deadly power of America's new **weapon of mass destruction.** (28)

World War II left the U.S. in a position of **political, economic** and **military superiority.** (29)

" We must set the pace and assume the responsibility of the **majority stockholder** in this **corporation known as the world.**"

Leo Welch, former Chairman of the Board, Standard Oil of New Jersey (now Exxon) 1946

The U.S. eagerly **assumed responsibility** for determining the economic policies and selecting the management of what it considered to be the **subsidiary companies** that made up the "**corporation known as the world.**"

But this didn't go over too well in many nations that considered themselves to be **sovereign countries.**

FUERA YANKIS

Boy, I never read about **any** of that stuff in **here!**

AMERICA Land of Freedom

Chapter 2

The "Cold War" and the Exploits of the Self-Proclaimed "World Policeman"

Go ahead — make my day!

World Cop

The United States, however, had to contend with the **Soviet Union**, which had also emerged from the Second World War as a **world power.** For the next 45 years, the world was caught up in a global turf battle between the "**two superpowers.**" The U.S. was always much stronger than its Soviet adversary, but both countries maintained huge military forces to defend and expand their own "**spheres of influence.**" The contention between the two powers was called the "**Cold War**" because they never directly engaged each other in battle. But the "Cold War" was marked by plenty of violence in other countries. Typically, the two superpowers lined up on **opposite sides** of every conflict.

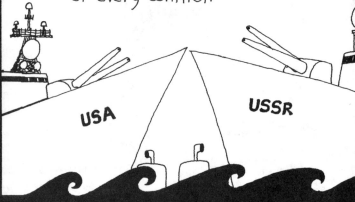

USA

USSR

For its part, the U.S. moved to expand its own "sphere of influence" beyond the Americas and the Pacific to include much of the **old British, French** and **Japanese colonial empires** in **Asia** and **Africa.** In doing so, it had to deal with local aspirations that did not always accord with American plans. To put down insubordination, disorder and disloyalty in its sphere, the new "**majority stockholder**" also appointed itself the "world policeman." During the Cold War, Washington **intervened** militarily in foreign countries more than **200 times.** (30)

Don't mess with the U.S.A., buster!

12

Korea, 1950-1953

After World War II, the **ambitious plans** of the U.S. State Department for Asia and the Pacific were upset completely by **revolutions and anti-colonial wars** from China to Malaysia. A major confrontation developed in **Korea**. Washington decided to intervene directly to show that **Western military technology** could defeat **any Asian army**.

We'll show these #@¿%$!

U.S. warships, bombers, and artillery reduced much of Korea to **rubble**. Over **4,500,000 Koreans died**; three out of four were **civilians**. **54,000 U.S. soldiers returned home in coffins.** But the U.S. military, for all of its technological superiority, **did not prevail.** After 3 years of intense warfare, a cease-fire was negotiated. Korea is still divided and some 40,000 U.S. troops remain in southern Korea to this day. (31)

Waiting for another war.

Dominican Republic, 1965

After a **U.S.-backed military coup,** Dominicans rose up to demand the reinstatement of the overthrown president (who they had elected in a popular vote). Washington, however, was determined to keep its men in power, **no matter who the Dominicans voted for.** 22,000 U.S. troops were sent to suppress the uprising. 3,000 people were **gunned down** in the streets of Santo Domingo. (32)

YANKEES GO HOME

Vietnam, 1964-1973

For ten years the U.S. assaulted Vietnam with all the deadly force the Pentagon could muster, trying to preserve a **corrupt South Vietnamese regime,** which had been inherited from the **French colonial empire.** The U.S. may have used **more firepower** in Indochina (Vietnam, Laos, and Cambodia) than had been used by **all sides** in all **previous wars** in human history.

> Sometimes you have to **destroy** a country to **save** it.

U.S. warplanes dropped **seven million tons** of bombs on Vietnam.

> That's the equivalent of one 350-pound bomb per **person!**

Despite the ferocity of the assault on Vietnam, the U.S. was ultimately defeated by a **lightly armed but determined** peasant army.

(33)

400,000 tons of napalm were rained down on the tiny country. **Agent Orange** and other toxic herbicides were used to destroy millions of acres of farmland and forests. Villages were burned to the ground and their residents massacred. Altogether, **two million people died** in the Indochina War, most of them civilians killed by U.S. bombs and bullets. Almost **60,000 U.S. soldiers were killed** and 300,000 wounded.

(14)

Lebanon, 1982-1983

After the Israeli invasion of Lebanon, the U.S. Marines intervened directly in the **Lebanese civil war**, taking the side of Israel and the right-wing Falange militia.

Which had just massacred 2000 Palestinian civilians.

U.S. Marines marching into Beirut, 1983

241 Marines paid for this intervention with their lives when their barracks were blown up by a **truck bomb.** (34)

Grenada, 1983

About **110,000 people** live on the tiny Caribbean island of **Grenada.**

About the same number that live in **Peoria, Illinois.**

But, according to **Ronald Reagan**, Grenada represented a ~~threat to U.S. security~~. So he ordered the Pentagon to seize the island and install a new government **more to his liking.** (35)

"A lovely piece of **real estate.**" (36)

Secretary of State George Schultz, 1983

I'm a Bechtel man and a Pentagon fan

Libya, 1986

Washington loved **King Idris**, the Libyan monarch who happily turned over his country's **oil reserves** to Standard Oil for **next to nothing**. It hates **Col. Qadhafi**, who threw the King out. In 1986, Reagan ordered U.S. warplanes to bomb the Libyan capital, Tripoli, claiming that Qadhafi was responsible for a bomb attack at a German disco that **killed two U.S. soldiers**. It's unlikely that very many of the hundreds of Libyans killed or injured in the U.S. bombing raid **knew anything** about the German bombing.

The nerve of those terrorists — **bombing** those poor people!

(37)

So far we've recounted wars that have **involved U.S. troops**.

But there are many **other wars** in which Washington is involved **behind the scenes**.

After World War II, Britain was compelled to dispose of its **colonial empire** in the Middle East. The British gave a big chunk of the land known as **Palestine** to **European Jews** displaced by the **Holocaust**. The problem was that there were already people living there. The result has been five decades of violence and war. Hundreds of thousands of Palestinians were **driven from their homes** in what became Israel. The center of the conflict has been the **West Bank** and **Gaza**, where Palestinians have lived for decades under **Israeli occupation**.

The U.S. provides crucial political support and billions of dollars a year in aid to Israel, including the most **advanced weaponry**. More than three decades of occupation of the West Bank and Gaza have produced bitter anger not only at Israel but also at the United States. As **Palestinian teenagers** continue to die in confrontations with the **Israeli Army** this anger only grows.

Made in USA

(38)

The U.S. government stands behind its friends -including dictatorial regimes suppressing their own people. In the 1970s and '80s **popular insurgencies** challenged corrupt dictatorships in **Central America**. The Pentagon and the CIA armed and trained security forces and death squads that killed hundreds of thousands of people, mostly **unarmed peasants**, in Nicaragua, El Salvador, and Guatemala.

(39)

Don't believe them - they were terrorists **disguised as peasants!**

Many of the military officers responsible for the **worst atrocities** in Central America were trained at the Pentagon's **"School of the Americas"** in Georgia. The School trains officers from all over Latin America. Its training manuals recommend **torture** and **summary execution**. Its graduates have returned to establish military regimes and **terrorize** their own people.

CLOSE the School of Assassins

NO MORE TORTURE TRAINING

(40)

Fort Benning is a Terrorist Training Camp

(41)

Today, bloody U.S.-backed counter-insurgency wars continue in **Colombia, Mexico, Peru,** the **Philippines** and other countries. In Colombia, a corrupt U.S.-backed army fights alongside paramilitary forces that have **slaughtered whole villages** and hundreds of opposition **union leaders** and **politicians**. The U.S. has been getting more deeply involved, under the cover of the **"War on Drugs,"** providing billions of dollars of arms used to continue the killing.

US US

(16)

The CIA and the Pentagon have also organized **proxy armies** to overthrow governments that are **not well-liked in Washington**. In 1961, for instance, U.S. warships ferried **a small army of mercenaries** to Cuba, hoping to reverse the **Cuban Revolution**. They landed at the **Bay of Pigs**.

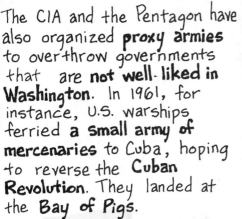

We'll show 'em!

Cubano

It was the **fifth U.S. invasion** of Cuba.
But this time the U.S. was **defeated**.

(42)

BOOM

In the 1970s and '80s, the **CIA** was **particularly busy** financing, training and arming **guerrilla armies** around the world

For years the U.S. backed Portugal's efforts to hang on to its **colonies in southern Africa**, helping it stave off independence wars in **Angola** and **Mozambique**.

In 1975, after a democratic revolution in Portugal, the Portuguese **called it quits**.

But Washington didn't!

Instead, it teamed up with the **apartheid regime** in South Africa to supply **a mercenary army** to fight the new government in independent Angola. And in Mozambique, top U.S. and South African politicians and ex-military officers sponsored a **particularly brutal bunch** of mercenaries who massacred tens of thousands of peasants.

(43)

Democracy!

Freedom!

USA

South African Apartheid Regime

And then, of course, there are the "contras."

After the **Nicaraguan people** overthrew the U.S.-backed dictatorship of the Somoza family in 1979, the CIA gathered together the **remnants of Somoza's hated National Guard** and sent them back to Nicaragua with all the weapons they could carry— to **loot, burn, and kill.**

"[The contras are] the **moral equivalent** of our founding fathers."

Ronald Reagan, 1985

I'm a contra too!

44

In 1979, the Soviet Union invaded **Afghanistan** to prop up a friendly regime. **Soviet occupation** met **fierce popular resistance.** The CIA stepped in to arm, finance and train the Afghan **mujahedin guerrillas,** working closely with the Pakistani and Saudi governments. With generous support from Washington and its allies, the mujahedin defeated the Soviets after a **brutal decade-long war.**

45

Among the CIA's collaborators in this war was a Saudi named **Osama bin Laden.** Together with the CIA, bin Laden supplied the Afghan mujahedin with money and guns to fight the Soviets. The Afghan war helped **militarize** an **international Islamic movement** to rid the Muslim world of foreign domination. Ultimately, this movement didn't like the **United States** any more than the **Soviets.** At that time, however, the U.S. backers of bin Laden and the mujahedin were not overly concerned about their wider goals.

46

We will drive **all infidel troops** from Muslim lands!

That's right! Let's whip the **Evil Empire!**

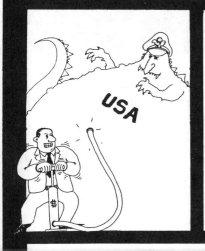

In the 1980s, Reagan **stepped up the arms race,** increasing military spending to unprecedented levels. The Soviets, with a much smaller economy, **struggled to keep up.**

Two can play **this** game!

USA

USSR

But they couldn't. Massive military spending put **tremendous strain** on Soviet society, contributing to its **collapse.** The U.S. **won the arms race** and the **Cold War.**

As the Cold War came to an end, some people began talking about an "**era of world peace**" and a "**peace dividend.**" But behind closed doors at the White House and the Pentagon the talk was quite different.

They were busy planning a **new era of wars**

We're the only superpower now!

NEW WORLD ORDER

Chapter 3
The
"New World Order"

In 1989, as the "Eastern Bloc" began to **crumble,** top U.S. government strategists gathered to discuss the **world situation.** The Soviet Union, they happily agreed, was no longer **able or inclined** to counter U.S. military intervention abroad. It was time, they decided, to **demonstrate U.S. military power** to the world. The White House wanted some **decisive victories.**

Much Weaker Enemy

Much Weaker Enemy

Yes!

Yes!

Yes!

"In cases where the U.S. confronts **much weaker enemies,** our challenge will be not simply to defeat them, but to defeat them **decisively and rapidly.**"

From a National Security Council policy review document, 1989

(47)

(19)

Panama, 1989

Panama was the first country selected to be the **"much weaker enemy."**

Ever since **U.S. warships** brought Panama into existence, U.S. troops have intervened in the small country whenever Washington deemed it necessary. George H.W. **Bush** continued this **tradition** in 1989, sending in **25,000 troops**.

Supposedly to arrest a drug dealer.

The drug charges were only a pretext. The real motive was assuring U.S. control over the **Panama Canal** and the extensive **U.S. military bases** in that country. A **new Panamanian president** was sworn in at a U.S. air base moments before the invasion. Hardly "Mr. Clean," the man the U.S. State Department picked for the job, Guillermo Endara, ran a bank that is notorious for **money laundering**.

(48)

We believe in **free enterprise!**

Of course, not only Panamanian banks are involved in this business. Most **big U.S. banks** have set up branches in Panama City.

(49)

Gotta get a piece of the action!

And drug trafficking and money laundering have **increased** sharply in Panama since **"Operation Just Cause."**

(50)

Aduana/ Customs

Cocaine

According to Panamanian human rights groups, **several thousand people were killed** in the U.S. invasion. 26 were U.S. soldiers. 50 were Panamanian soldiers. The rest were **civilians,** cut down by the overwhelming U.S. firepower poured into **crowded neighborhoods** in poor sections of Panama City and Colón. ⑤¹

Many of the dead were put in **garbage bags** and **secretly buried** in mass graves.

Iraq, 1991

Only 13 months after the invasion of Panama, the U.S. went to war again — this time on a much **larger scale.** The 1991 U.S.-Iraq War continued an **epic battle** for control over the **immensely rich oil fields** of the Persian Gulf that began over 75 years earlier.

During World War I, the British conquered the region that is now Iraq and Kuwait, **seizing** it from the **declining Ottoman Empire.**

We didn't **conquer** the Arabs—we **liberated** them!

In 1920 hundreds of British soldiers and many more Iraqis died when the British Army suppressed a **revolt** against **British rule.** Britain ended up installing a **hand-picked** **"King of Iraq."** The new monarch promptly signed a deal with British and American oil companies giving them the right to **exploit all of Iraq's oil** for 75 years in exchange for a pittance in royalties.

⑤²

God save the **King!**

As the British Empire declined, the U.S. became the **senior partner** in an enduring **Anglo-American alliance.** The Middle East became a key part of their global "sphere of influence."

The Middle East possesses almost **two-thirds** of the **world's known oil reserves.** Control over the flow of oil by U.S. and British companies gave Washington **strategic power** over Europe, Japan and the developing world. The U.S. State Department declared that Middle Eastern oil was...

(53)

"...a stupendous source of **strategic power**... one of the **greatest prizes** in world history"

Washington came to think of the oil fields in the Middle East as its own **private reserves.**

(54)

What are you up to?

Exploring to see if there are any **vital American interests** under your soil

Mobil

In 1958, U.S. and British oil companies were startled when the **King of Iraq** was **overthrown.** The new leader, a nationalist military officer named Abdel Karim Qasim, demanded changes in the **sweetheart deals** the monarchy had made with the oil companies. He also helped form **OPEC**, the cartel of oil producing countries.

Besides, the guy was consorting with communists!

CIA

In 1963, the **CIA** collaborated with the **Ba'ath Party** to **murder** Qasim and overthrow his government. The Ba'ath Party was also nationalist but at least it was **anti-communist.** It systematically killed its Leftist opponents and the CIA was **happy to help.**

These Ba'ath guys are **efficient.** We give them lists of suspected communists and they get the **job done!**

(55)

CIA

Among the CIA's collaborators in the 1963 coup was a young military officer named **Saddam Hussein,** who later emerged as the top leader in Iraq.

But Hussein soon disappointed his accomplices in the U.S. by **nationalizing** the **Iraqi oil industry**. Other Arab leaders followed suit, greatly **alarming** U.S. officials. 56

"**Oil** is much **too important** a commodity to be **left in the hands** of the **Arabs**"

Henry Kissinger

Then, in 1980, Hussein did something that made him much **more popular** in Washington.

I decided to **invade** Iran!

U.S. officials were **delighted**. After the 1979 Iranian Revolution, American strategists considered **Iran** the **main threat** to U.S. interests in the Middle East. The U.S. and its allies, therefore, were happy to provide Hussein with **advanced weaponry**. U.S. companies even sold Iraq materials to make **chemical** and **biological weapons**, including highly lethal strains of **anthrax**. 57

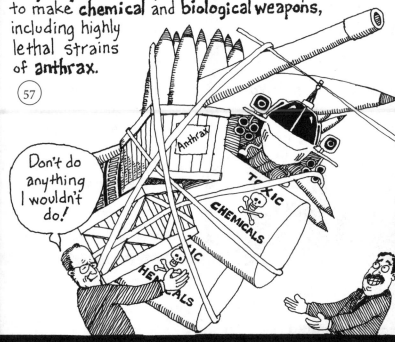

Don't do anything I wouldn't do!

Iraq used chemical weapons against both **Iranian troops** and **insurgent Kurdish villagers** inside Iraq. The Reagan Administration knew this, but the U.S. continued to supply Hussein not only with the necessary chemicals, but also with **satellite photos** of the positions of Iranian troops. Over 100,000 Iranian soldiers were killed or injured by **poison gas**. 58

In 1987, the Reagan administration intervened directly in the Iran-Iraq War (on Iraq's side), sending a **naval armada** to the Persian Gulf to protect the oil tankers of a country that was then Iraq's ally — Kuwait. Using state-of-the-art weaponry, the U.S. Navy blew up an Iranian **oil platform**, destroyed several **small speedboats**, and recklessly shot down an Iranian **passenger airliner**, killing all **290 passengers**. 59

We had to defend our ship!

Sure, what were they going **to do**, flush their toilets on you?

Despite U.S. support, Saddam Hussein failed to seize any of Iran's oilfields, so he then turned his attention to the **oilfields** of his **southern neighbor.**

I decided to **invade** Kuwait!

Hussein apparently expected that the U.S. would also tacitly go along with his invasion of Kuwait. For the U.S., however, Kuwait was **very different** from Iran. The **Kuwaiti emir** was a **loyal friend** of the U.S. and British oil companies and a close political ally of the United States. George H.W. Bush worried that the huge Iraqi army had become a threat to U.S. domination of the Middle East.

" **Our jobs, our way of life,** our own freedom, and the freedom of friendly countries around the world would all suffer if **control** of the **world's great oil reserves** fell into the hands of Saddam Hussein"

George H.W. Bush, August 1990

Bush decided Hussein had to be **punished** for trespassing on an **oil-rich U.S. protectorate.**

" **He's going to get his ass kicked!** "

The Honorable George H.W. Bush, December 1990

The war had a **message** for the world:

The Pentagon launched the **most intensive bombing campaign** in history using conventional bombs, **cluster bombs** (designed to rip bodies apart), **napalm** and **phosphorous** (which cling to and burn skin), and **fuel-air** explosives (which have the impact of small nuclear bombs). Later, the U.S. used munitions tipped with **depleted uranium,** which is now suspected as a cause of **cancer** among both Iraqis and U.S. soldiers and their children. Iraq was bombed back to a **pre-industrial age** and tens of thousands were killed.

Nuke Baghdad!

"What we say goes!"

AMERICA IS NO. 1 —AND DON'T YOU FORGET IT!

George H.W. Bush, February 1991

24

Baghdad and Basra were **bombed relentlessly,** killing thousands of civilians. (64)

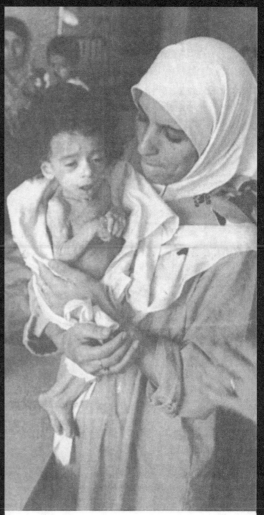

Iraq had already begun to withdraw from Kuwait when Bush launched the ground war. The main aim of the ground offensive was, in fact, **not** to drive the Iraqi troops out of Kuwait, but to **keep them from leaving.** The "**gate was closed**" and tens of thousands of soldiers, who were trying to go home, were **systematically slaughtered.** Elsewhere, U.S. tanks and bulldozers intentionally **buried thousands of soldiers alive** in their trenches in a tactic designed mainly to "destroy Iraqi defenders." (65)

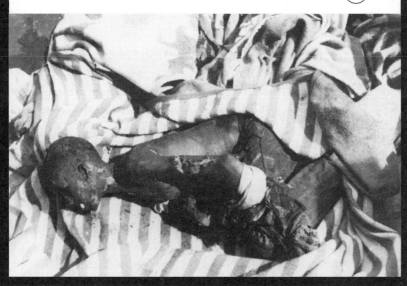

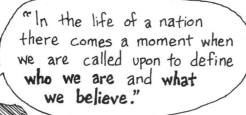

"In the life of a nation there comes a moment when we are called upon to define **who we are** and **what we believe.**" (66)

George H. Bush
January 1991

Tens of thousands of Iraqis died during the war. And the tragedy continued after the war ended. Even more people died from **water-borne diseases** that spread because the U.S. systematically destroyed Iraq's **electrical, sewage treatment** and **water treatment** systems. For over a decade, the U.S. insisted on maintaining the most **severe economic sanctions** regime in history, continuing to strangle the devastated Iraqi economy, with dire consequences for the Iraqi people. (67)

In 1999, **UNICEF** estimated that **infant and child mortality** had more than doubled since the war. It attributed this sharp increase in mortality mainly to malnutrition and deteriorating health conditions caused by the **war** and **ongoing sanctions**. It estimated that **half a million more children died** as a result. That's 5,200 children a month. (68)

That ought to **teach Saddam a lesson** he won't soon forget!

Have a Nice War

Bush's successsor, Bill Clinton, not only kept up the **sanctions**, but also continued to **bomb** Iraq regularly for **8 years**.

And the U.S. war on Iraq was **far from over**

Kosovo, 1999

In the late 1990s, after enduring **years of abuse** at the hands of a Serbian-dominated Yugoslav government, Albanian rebels in Kosovo started a **war for secession**. The U.S. usually does not support minority groups demanding separation. But it **all depends** on whether the U.S. supports the government of the country facing dismemberment. For instance, the U.S. supports **Kurdish separatists** in **Iraq and Iran**, but across the border in **Turkey**, a close ally, Washington has provided tons of arms to **crush the Kurds.** With U.S. help, tens of thousands have been killed. (69)

Our policy is clear— We support people **fighting** for their **freedom** and oppose **terrorist separatists**

US   US

Because the **Yugoslav strongman**, Slobodan Milosevic, was being less than cooperative with U.S. efforts to extend its influence in Eastern Europe, **breaking up Yugoslavia** was a cause the U.S. could warm up to. The Clinton Administration embraced the Kosovo Liberation Army, despite their **drug dealing, ethnic extremism** and **brutality.** Following established practice, the Administration issued an ultimatum the Yugoslavs **could not possibly accept.** (70)

Here's the deal. First, **NATO** takes over Kosovo. Second, **NATO** has free access to all of Yugoslavia. Third, you help pay for the **NATO-run** government. **Sign here or we bomb you.**

The NATO bombing turned an ugly but small-scale Yugoslav counter-insurgency operation into a massive **ethnic cleansing** drive. After the bombing began, Serbian soldiers and militia members began driving hundreds of thousands of Albanians out of the country and killed thousands of others. When the **Albanians** returned under NATO protection, **Serbian** and **Gypsy** residents were driven out and killed. Ultimately, the war served **U.S. political objectives**, while causing tremendous death and suffering on all sides and greatly **aggravating ethnic antagonisms.** (71)

Chapter 4
The
"War on Terrorism"

After the horrific **September 11 terrorist attacks** on the World Trade Center and the Pentagon, **one question** was so **sensitive** it was seldom seriously addressed by the U.S. news media.

Mom, **why** did they **do it?**

To find out, it makes sense to ask the **prime suspect** himself. As U.S. warplanes began bombing Afghanistan, **Osama bin Laden** released a videotaped message. He **praised** the **September 11 attacks** and called for more attacks on the United States. Then he spelled out his **motivations** quite clearly.

" What America is tasting now is something insignificant compared to what we have tasted for scores of years. Our nation (the Islamic world) has been tasting this **humiliation** and **degradation** for more than **80 years.** Its sons are killed, its **blood is shed**, its sanctuaries are attacked and no one hears and no one heeds. Millions of innocent children are being killed as I speak. They are being killed in **Iraq** without committing any sins.... To **America,** I say only a few words to it and its people. I swear to God, who has elevated the skies without pillars, **neither America nor the people** who live in it will **dream of security** before we live it here in **Palestine** and not before all the **infidel armies leave the land of Muhammad**, peace be upon him." (72)

Osama bin Laden Oct. 7, 2001

Few people anywhere in the world, including the Middle East, support bin Laden's terrorist methods. But most people in the Middle East **share his anger** at the United States. They are angry at the U.S. for supporting **corrupt** and **dictatorial regimes** in the region, for **supporting Israel** at the expense of the Palestinians and for imposing **U.S. dictates** on the Middle East through **military might** and **brutal economic sanctions**.

The Bush Administration immediately instructed U.S. television networks to **"exercise caution"** in airing bin Laden's taped messages. The official reason?

The tapes may contain **secret coded messages** for terrorist operatives

But were **covert messages** the Administration's main concern? Perhaps it was more worried about the impact of bin Laden's **overt message** - that the **September 11** attacks were carried out in **retaliation** for U.S. foreign policy and particularly **U.S. military intervention** in the Middle East.

If Americans realized that U.S. military intervention abroad brought retaliation - causing **death and destruction at home** - we might **think twice** about whether the U.S. should be so **eager to go to war** overseas

The Pentagon has demonstrated time and again that its advanced weaponry can **devastate countries** targeted for attack, **leveling** basic **infrastructure** and **killing thousands**, even hundreds of thousands of people.

It would be **naive** to think there would be **no retaliation**

Over the last several decades the **true costs** of the wars the U.S. has waged overseas have been largely **hidden**. We have had to **pay the military bills** but few Americans have died. The **death** and **destruction** were all **overseas**. That changed on **September 11**.

The **violence reached the United States**

The September 11 attacks, however, were not simply acts of **retribution**. They were also **provocation**. Bin Laden expected the U.S. to respond with **massive violence**, knowing this would bring him **new recruits**. Ultimately, he hoped to win the majority of the Muslim world to support his **holy war on the U.S.**

More **martyrs**, more **recruits!**

The Bush Administration responded according to **bin Laden's script**. George W. Bush declared a "**War on Terrorism**," using "good vs. evil" rhetoric that mirrored bin Laden's. Bush and his advisors were ready - **even eager** - for the war bin Laden wanted. They saw the September 11 attacks as a **grand opportunity** to boost military spending and demonstrate U.S. military power to the world.

(73)

"This will be a monumental struggle of **good versus evil** ... This **crusade**, this **war on terrorism**, is going to take a while"

George W. Bush
September 12 and 16, 2001

The self-righteous "**good vs. evil**" rhetoric of the "War on Terrorism" sharpens ironies that have long shadowed U.S. pronouncements against **state-sponsored terrorism**. President Bush, for instance, promised to scour the globe in search of **states** that **harbor terrorists**.

He could have started in the **State of Florida**

What do you mean?

For over forty years, **Miami** has served as the base of operations for well-financed groups of **Cuban exiles** that have carried out violent **terrorist attacks on Cuba**.

Most recently, they **bombed** a number of Havana tourist spots in 1997, killing an Italian tourist, and they tried to **assassinate** Fidel Castro in Panama in 2000.

(29)

It would not be difficult for the U.S. government to find evidence involving these terrorist organizations because the **CIA** and the **Pentagon trained** many of their **members**. Take, for instance, **Luis Posada Carriles** and **Orlando Bosch**, suspected masterminds of the **bombing** of a **Cuban passenger airliner** that claimed the lives of **73 people**. (74)

"All of Castro's planes are **warplanes**"

Orlando Bosch, 1987, defending the bombing of the civilian Cuban plane

Before Posada Carriles could be tried for the airline bombing, he **escaped** from a **prison** in Venezuela and found a job **supplying arms** to the CIA-backed **Nicaraguan Contras**.

My **experience** in the **CIA** gave me the **right credentials** for the job (75)

Posada's accomplice, Orlando Bosch, has long been **protected from extradition** by the U.S. goverment. Although Bosch was convicted of carrying out a **bazooka attack** on a ship in **Miami harbor**, President George H.W. Bush –at the urging of his son Jeb – prevented his expulsion from the country. Bush signed an **executive pardon** providing Bosch with **safe haven** in Florida. Bosch promised to...

"Rejoin **the struggle!**" (76) (77)

Hold on! Let me set the record straight. I **pardon only freedom fighters**, not terrorists!

If George W. Bush had been serious about going after **all** states that **harbor terrorists**, he would have issued an **ultimatum** to **his brother,** the governor of Florida.

Listen Jeb, you're going to have to **cough up** the terrorists or we start **bombing Miami** tomorrow!

Posada, Bosch and their friends are **only a few** of the violent characters whose activities have been sponsored by the CIA. Many of the CIA's **"covert operations"** – bombings, **assassinations, sabotage,** and **paramilitary massacres** – are terrorism by any definition. Many of the shadowy figures involved in these activities are still working with the CIA around the world. But others – including **Osama bin Laden** – have turned on their former American partners. (78)

It's **too bad.** They made such a **good team.**

Afghanistan, 2001 - ?

Bush's **"War on Terrorism"** began with U.S. warplanes **bombing Afghanistan**, the unfortunate country where bin Laden chose to locate his headquarters. At that time, Afghanistan was ruled by fundamentalist Muslim clerics of the Taliban movement, whom both bin Laden and the CIA had supported during the anti-Soviet war. Now, Washington decided to **destroy its former allies**.

The people of Afghanistan suffered the consequences

Americans were mobilized for war with calls for **vengeance**.

(79)

U.S. special forces officer, Afghanistan February 2002

*"We will **export death and violence** to the four corners of the earth in defense of our great nation!"*

The U.S. made common cause with a new set of Afghan allies – **brutal regional warlords.** Under U.S. auspices, Islamic fundamentalism was replaced with brazen corruption as warlords fought for power and **preyed on people** under their jurisdiction. The **opium trade**, which zealous Taliban clerics had briefly suppressed, once again flourished under **warlord protection**.

(81)

Within a year, U.S. warplanes had killed **more civilians** than had died in the World Trade Center. And the bombing went on for **years to come**. (80)

And Afghanistan regained its place as the **world's top opium producer**

Relatives prepare four children for burial after a U.S. air strike in Kabul. October 2001

Bush thought he could make **quick work** of the Taliban, install a **pro-U.S. regime**, and move on. Things didn't work out that way.

Fifteen years later, over **2300 American soldiers had died** and the U.S. was still fighting in Afghanistan

(82)

31

Iraq, 2003 - 2011

From the day they took office, Bush and his key lieutenants **set their sights on Iraq**. After 9-11, they packaged an invasion as part of the "War on Terrorism." To win U.N. backing, they claimed Saddam Hussein was developing **nuclear, chemical,** and **biological weapons**. The threat was so **imminent**, they said, that an immediate invasion was **imperative**. (83)

"We can't **wait** for the final proof – the smoking gun – that could come in the form of a **mushroom cloud**"

George W. Bush
October 2002

But the spector of "weapons of mass destruction" was just a **pretext**. Bush, therefore, had little use for **U.N. weapons inspectors** in Iraq.

Get those *%&# inspectors out of the way– I'm getting ready to **bomb the place!**

The U.N. refused to endorse the invasion but the U.S. and Britain **went ahead anyway**. The Iraqi Army was **decimated** and thousands of Iraqi civilians were also killed. (84)

As soon as U.S. troops captured Baghdad, elated American officials began **issuing threats** to Iraq's neighbors, Syria and Iran. The message was: Go along with the American program **or else...**

(85)

"This doesn't mean, **necessarily**, that other governments have to fall. They can **moderate their behavior**"

Senior U.S. official, April 2003

Bush declared that the U.S. had **liberated** the people of Iraq

And we're gonna bring 'em **democracy, too!**

But it soon became clear that "liberation" came with **strings attached**.

U.S. Secretary of State Colin Powell, April 2003

"We didn't take on this huge burden not to have **significant, dominating control**"

(86)

The U.S. was in no hurry to hold elections. Bush appointed Paul Bremer III to head up the U.S. occupation authority. Instead of popular elections, Bremer proposed that a new governing assembly be selected by **handpicked** "**caucuses**."

"In a post-war situation like this, if you start holding elections, the people who are **rejectionists** tend to win"

Paul Bremer III
June 2003

(87)

By "rejectionists" Bremer meant those who oppose U.S. occupation

Bremer named Philip Carroll, former chief of the U.S. division of **Shell Oil**, to take charge of the Iraqi oil industry, and Peter McPherson, a former **Bank of America** executive, to run Iraq's Central Bank. U.S. military officers were placed in charge of Iraqi cities.

(88)

We call it the **corporate-military model** of government

Actually, the main thing the U.S. wanted to **liberate** was **Iraqi oil**. Before the war the Iraqi oil industry was controlled by state-owned companies. Western oil companies were **shut out** and they were **not happy**.

"Iraq possesses **huge reserves of gas and oil** — reserves I'd love Chevron to have **access** to"

Kenneth Derr
Chevron CEO
1998

(89)

As soon as Baghdad fell, U.S. officials and representatives of U.S. oil companies were busy writing a **new Hydrocarbon Law** that would **privatize** the Iraqi oil industry and give concessions to foreign companies on very favorable terms.

Now it's a whole new ballgame!

-click

(90)

When Bush was preparing the public to go to war, he was carefull **never to mention** the word **oil**. But the general in charge of U.S. occupation forces was more forthright.

"**Of course, it's about oil.** We can't really deny that."

Gen. John Abizaid
former commander of
U.S. military operations
in Iraq, 2007

(91)

But the war was not only about oil. Bush and his advisers wanted to establish **a U.S. client regime** in Iraq as a base of operations for an ambitious effort to **remake the entire Middle East.** (92)

That's **America's job,** isn't it?

But Bush overlooked **one detail** — that the people of Iraq might not go along with his plans!

Iraq's leading Shiite cleric, Grand Ayatollah Ali al-Sistani, mobilized huge demonstrations demanding **direct popular elections** and an end to U.S. military occupation.

Others **took up arms** against the occupiers. Bush's response was more swaggering cowboy talk.

"There are some who feel like... they can attack us there. My answer is — **bring them on!**"

George W. Bush, Washington, DC July 2003 (93)

Bush sent in more troops and the occupation of Iraq followed the familiar path of previous **ill-fated colonial adventures.** As Iraqis organized armed resistance — with wide popular support — the U.S. military took increasingly harsh **punitive measures** against the population, inspiring fear and indignation.

"They can make it easy on themselves and tell us who the bums are and we'll go search them out, or they will be **subjected to some pain.** But we are not going to tolerate attacks on coalition forces and people **jumping for joy** in the streets."

Major General Charles Swannock, Jr. November 2003 (referring to the population of the city of Fallujah) (94)

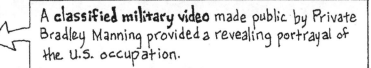
A **classified military video** made public by Private Bradley Manning provided a revealing portrayal of the U.S. occupation.

The video, shot from an Apache helicopter gunsight, recorded the **unprovoked killing** of over a dozen Iraqis including two Reuters journalists in Baghdad in 2007. In this still, rescuers are shot while helping the wounded. (95)

Tens of thousands of Iraqis **disappeared** into prisons run by the U.S. military. Prisoners were held without charge and were subjected to **humiliation, sexual abuse,** and **torture.**

(96)

"Now all Iraqis can **taste liberty** in their native land!"

(97)

U.S. Attorney General John Ashcroft after he sent a team to rebuild Iraq's system of courts and prisons in 2003

Early on it was clear that Bush's grandiose plans had **gone awry.**

"**They** don't want us here and **we** don't want to be here"

(98)

Unidentified American soldier, Baghdad June 2003

But for **eight years** the U.S. **pushed on,** with Obama taking over where Bush left off. When the U.S. finally withdrew from Iraq in 2011, it left **empty handed.** It had failed to install a **puppet regime.** Instead the new government was closer to Iran than to the U.S. Washington had failed to secure permanent military bases in Iraq and due to widespread public opposition the Iraqi Parliament had **refused to pass** the U.S.-sponsored **Hydrocarbon Law.**

(99)

Ingrates!

Iraq and Syria, 2014 - ?

Don't worry, this time we're **only** bombing!

In 2014 the U.S. went to war for a **third time** in Iraq and expanded the campaign to Syria. The target, **ISIS**, emerged out of the **chaos** created by the U.S. invasion of Iraq and flourished as a result of U.S. efforts to topple the Syrian regime. American efforts to **reshape the Middle East by force** have been disastrous - and at this point there's **no end in sight.**

The costs of these wars- from Afghanistan to Iraq- have been enormous. More than **6,800** U.S. soldiers have **lost their lives** more than **52,000** have been **wounded**, and hundreds of thousands suffer from **PTSD**.

And for **what?**

The wars have cost U.S. taxpayers more than **$4.3 trillion**, not counting the future costs of veterans care and interest on the war debt — which might reach **$7.9 trillion**.

The costs have been far greater for Afghans and Iraqis. By one calculation, **113,000 civilians** have been killed by U.S. forces in Iraq alone.

Thousands more have been killed in Afghanistan but nobody knows how many

And both countries have been left in **shambles**

After the disastrous experiences in Afghanistan and Iraq, many people were hoping the U.S. might **take a break** from global warmaking.

But **addiction** is hard to break

Obama's Drone Wars

Under the Obama Administration, the U.S. has granted itself a liscence to use **remotely controlled planes** to kill people at its discretion around the world.

They don't call me the **technology president** for nothing!

Following Bush's experiments with militarized drones, Obama has turned drones into a **major new form of warfare**. The U.S. is setting up a **global network of drone bases** from which to launch strikes on **suspected enemies**. U.S. drones have already killed thousands of people in Pakistan, Yemen, and Somalia, including hundreds of civilians, many of them children. ⑩²

Three Pakistani children orphaned a few hours earlier by a **CIA drone strike** that killed their parents and siblings, 2010

For now, only the U.S., the U.K. and Israel conduct drone strikes, but this **monopoly won't last.** Scores of countries are rushing to add drones to their arsenals.

What happens when they all begin to **send out drones** to assassinate people?

The U.S. is pioneering a new type of warfare in which the killing is done by **remote control**. This is **lowering the threshold of war.** When political leaders can dispatch robots rather than soldiers, it will be much easier to go to war.

⑩³

Looming on the horizon is an era of **warfare without beginning or end** and without defined borders

U.S. politicians claim that drone strikes will **curb terrorism.** They said the same thing about the wars in Afghanistan and Iraq. But just the opposite is true. The invasions of Afghanistan and Iraq and the deployment of drones to patrol the skies of Muslim countries have only added fuel to **simmering anti-American sentiments** and spurred more attacks.

USA
THE REAL TERRORIST

The **spiral of bloodshed** is escalating dangerously. America's long-time **addiction to war** has reached a **new level,** creating greater dangers for people in this country and around the world.

Unfortunately, there are some people who **profit handsomely** from this addiction...

Chapter 5

The War Profiteers

In the front lines of the **pro-war crowd** you'll find an assortment of **politicians, generals,** and **corporate executives**. If you ask them why they are so eager to go to war they'll give you **noble** and **selfless** reasons.

But what **really motivates** them to go to war are **somewhat less lofty** aims:

For **most** people, the huge Pentagon budget means **less money** in their pockets.

IRS

PENTAGON

But for **some** people, just the opposite is true.

War Profits

Over 100,000 companies feed at the Pentagon trough. But the **big money** goes to a handful of huge corporations.

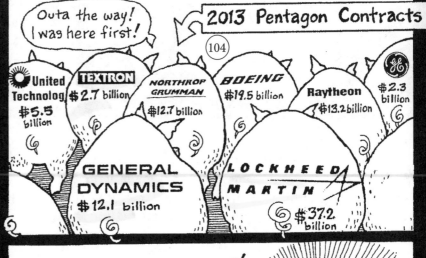

Outa the way! I was here first!

2013 Pentagon Contracts

(104)

United Technolog $5.5 billion

TEXTRON $2.7 billion

NORTHROP GRUMMAN $12.7 billion

BOEING $19.5 billion

Raytheon $13.2 billion

GE $2.3 billion

GENERAL DYNAMICS $12.1 billion

LOCKHEED MARTIN $37.2 billion

As they watch **missiles flying** and the **bombs dropping** in the Middle East, top executives of the big weapons manufacturers are adding up their profits, their brains working like **cash registers gone haywire.**

ch-ching

ch-ching

For weapons makers, wars mean more orders — not only from the Pentagon, but also from overseas. After the first Gulf War demonstrated that their weapons can truly **kill on a massive scale**, foreign sales by U.S. weapons manufacturers **skyrocketed.**

(105)

We've got a **real deal** on F-16's this week — buy 100 and **we'll throw in** 1,000 cases of **napalm free!**

FREE NAPALM OFFER! We overstocked! Gulf tested! Gulf proven! Kill like you never have before!

Our weapons kill:
• more
• better
• faster

Who are the war profiteers?

"Let's take a look at some of the men in Washington who are most **gung ho** about war..."

Dick Cheney

Few politicians can match Dick Cheney's **enthusiasm for war** - or his record of **wanton destruction**. As George H.W. Bush's Secretary of Defense he presided over wars against Panama and Iraq, and then as Vice President under George W. Bush, he led the war drives against Afghanistan and Iraq.

Between wars, Dick has turned his attention from **destruction** to **construction** - that is post-war reconstruction. In 1995, he was named CEO of **Halliburton**, the world's largest oil services company and a major military contractor. After the first Gulf War, Halliburton was hired to help rebuild the Kuwaiti oil industry. Then after the second Gulf War, the company was back to **clean up the mess again** - for a **healthy fee**. (106)

Halliburton

"You've gotta hand it to Dick. He's got an **innovative business strategy** - first bomb it, then clean it up, then bomb it again, then clean it up again!"

Halliburton was awarded **secret no-bid contracts** even before the war began and it raked in tens of billions of dollars in Iraq feeding and housing U.S. troops and **rebuilding oil facilities**. (107)

"It's **nice** to have friends in Washington!"

As Halliburton's CEO, Cheney was **rewarded handsomely**, pocketing millions in salary and stock options every year. He ended up as Halliburton's largest individual stockholder, with a $45 million stake. (108)

"I **earned** every penny of it!"

Cheney got **draft deferments** five times to avoid fighting in Vietnam. But he's eager to send **others** to **fight and die**, and then **reap the benefits**. He's served on the boards of several huge war contractors, and his wife - Lynne - joined the board of Lockheed Martin. After Cheney returned to the White House in 2001, Lockheed got the **biggest plum** in Pentagon history - a contract worth hundreds of billions to make the next generation of fighter jets.

(109)

"We're just doing our **patriotic duty**!"

Richard Perle

As head of the Pentagon's Defense Policy Board, Richard Perle was a **chief architect** of both the **war on Iraq** and Donald Rumsfeld's efforts to "**revolutionize**" military technology. In 2001, Perle joined Henry Kissinger and other **Washington insiders** to form a company called Trireme Partners. Trireme raises **venture capital** from wealthy individuals and invests it in weapons companies, betting on those it expects will get lucrative government contracts. (110)

Insider trading? We prefer to call it **guaranteed speculation!**

Henry

Perle has also served as an advisor to the **Israeli government**. Whether in Washington or Jerusalem, his advice is always the same...

War is **the answer!**

Perle has particularly pushed for war against three countries he considers Israel's main enemies - **Iraq, Iran** and **Syria**.

One down, **two to go!** (111)

Cheney, Perle and their friends go back and forth through a **revolving door** that connects jobs at the Pentagon, the White House, Congress and corporate military contractors. Lots of **money changes hands** in Washington as weapons manufacturers make **generous contributions** to politicians and politicians hand out **fat Pentagon contracts** to weapons manufacturers. This leads to all kinds of **shady agreements** and **overpriced goods**.

Here's to the Pentagon – the only place you can sell a 13¢ bolt for $2,043! (112)

The "War on Terrorism" has led to a tremendous **windfall** for the military contractors. The Army, Navy, and Air Force (and the contractors they represent) are lining up to get money for **expensive new weapons systems**, now packaged as indispensable for fighting terrorism.

We **can't afford** to be without it!

It's **vital** for **homeland defense!**

We have to close the **window of vulnerability!**

Even Congressional opposition to the far-fetched "missile defense program" collapsed.

Beep Beep

Missile defense, like the "War on Terrorism," **promises to protect Americans** from danger while actually creating a much **more dangerous world**. If other countries think there is any chance the U.S. could block their missiles, they will feel **vulnerable** to U.S. attack. China has already promised to build more and better missiles which could overwhelm the U.S. "missile shield." This will spur a **nuclear arms race in Asia**.

If **China** builds more nuclear missiles, then **India** will. If India does, then **Pakistan** will. If Pakistan...

In 1972, the U.S. and the U.S.S.R. signed the **ABM Treaty** to try to avoid this kind of arms race. In order to pursue missile defense, the U.S. **unilaterally scrapped** the treaty. But that didn't bother missile defense proponents.

(113)

Hey, the world's changed. **We can win an arms race** with anyone!

In this spirit, Congress **rejected** the **nuclear test ban treaty** (which has been signed by 164 countries) and it continues to finance nuclear weapons research and production. In fact, the Pentagon is eager to develop a new arsenal of small "**battlefield**" nuclear weapons.

(114)

The U.S. is keeping enough nuclear firepower to **wipe out** most of **humanity**.

Just to be safe!

As potential nuclear targets in Russia have declined, the Pentagon has been retargeting its missiles at "**every reasonable adversary**."

Which makes other countries feel like they better **hurry up** and get nuclear weapons themselves

(115)

In the post-Cold War world order, the U.S. does not seem to want to be bound by any arms treaties. It **refuses to sign** a new protocol to the 1972 biological weapons treaty because it would require **international inspections** of its **biological weapons research facilities**, where it is creating **deadly new strains** including highly lethal **powdered anthrax**. U.S. officials say they are only creating germ weapons in order to study how to defend against them.

(116)

Of course, we would **never** use them **ourselves!**

But can other countries **trust** a government that bombed Hiroshima and Nagasaki and actually developed plans to use **smallpox** and other biological weapons against **Vietnam** and **Cuba?**

(117)

Would you?

And U.S. **"weaponized germs"** not only represent a threat to people in other countries.

What if some of the Pentagon's powdered anthrax got into the hands of **some fanatic here** in the United States?

During the Cold War, the Soviet Union was a serious military competitor for the United States. Today, the U.S. maintains a huge war machine despite the **lack of any serious competition.** The U.S. military budget is now larger than the next ten biggest spenders **put together!** It makes up a full **37%** of **total global military spending.**

United States $640 billion

Annual Military Expenditures
2013

China $188 billion

Russia $88 billion

Saudi Arabia $67 billion

Being the **world cop** and all, we do have certain responsibilities!

(118)

If we add up the current Pentagon budget, the **nuclear weapons budget** of the Energy Department, the **Homeland Security budget**, the cost of military retirement and **veterans care**, the military share of **interest payments** on the national debt, etc., the U.S. spends over a **trillion dollars** a year to keep up its military machine.

Trillion dollars a year
$109,000,000,000
Total military-related budget
Fiscal year 2015

That's almost **two million** dollars a **minute!**

(120)

This **costs you plenty.** With more than half of our income taxes going to military spending, most American families end up contributing **thousands of dollars a year** to feed the Pentagon's addiction.

While we're struggling to **make ends meet!**

Mom- could we get...

If you need anything else, just **give a holler!**

Because Congress is so **generous to the Pentagon...**

Social programs get **short changed**

That's all we can afford - we can't **bust the budget,** you know.

Bridges, roads, sewers, and water systems are **crumbling** because the government fails to provide the money needed to maintain them.

(121)

°o(!?)

CREAK

Bus fares are rising and **service** is being **slashed** as the Federal Government has eliminated financial support for mass transit operating costs.

(122)

NOT IN SERVICE

Be all you can be in the Army!

RTA

Schools are **run-down** and over-crowded. In some inner-city high schools, 80% of the students drop out. More than a fifth of all adults **can't read** a job application or a street sign. Yet federal education funding per student has declined substantially over the last two decades.

(123)

We believe in **bake sale** financing.

The **price of health care** continues to rise and holes in Obamacare have left tens of millions without adequate insurance. Yet public hospitals are being closed for **lack of funding.**

(124)

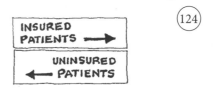

INSURED PATIENTS ⟶

UNINSURED ⟵ PATIENTS

EXIT

Mom, it hurts!

Reception

One-fifth of all **expectant mothers** do not receive **pre-natal care.** This is one reason the U.S. has the highest infant mortality rate in the developed world (twice as high as Japan's). **Every 50 minutes,** a child in the U.S. dies as a result of **poverty or hunger.** Yet Congress has been exceedingly stingy in funding maternal and child health programs.

(125)

I just **love** babies!

Why don't you put your **money** where your **mouth** is, mister?

Yuck!

Vote for Me!

With **rents rising** and **wages falling,** millions of families are living on the verge of eviction. Millions of people end up **living on the streets.** Yet when it comes to funding for housing and homelessness, most of Washington seems to have adopted Reagan's attitude.

(126)

Those people **want** to live on the streets!

Drug addiction and alcoholism are crippling millions of people, and devastating families and whole communities. Yet there are not enough public treatment centers to handle **even a fraction** of those seeking help, and many centers are **closing their doors** for lack of funding.

There's just **no money!**

Oh yeah?

Somehow you come up with billions of dollars a year to operate **12 aircraft carrier battle groups!**

With the $1,000,000,000 it takes to maintain just one of those aircraft carriers for a year, you could build **17,000 homes** for 67,000 people

(127)

...or you could provide **free prenatal care** for 1,600,000 expectant mothers, saving thousands of babies

(128)

...or enroll 384,000 more kids in the **Head Start** preschool program this year

(129)

...or provide intensive **drug or alcohol treatment** for 333,000 people

(130)

The **price of militarism** includes more than high taxes and poor social services. Building nuclear weapons, for instance, has probably been the **biggest environmental disaster** this country has ever seen. More than 100 nuclear weapons plants owned by the Energy Department have been **spewing radioactive waste** into the air, dumping it in rivers, and leaking it into the soil and groundwater for decades.

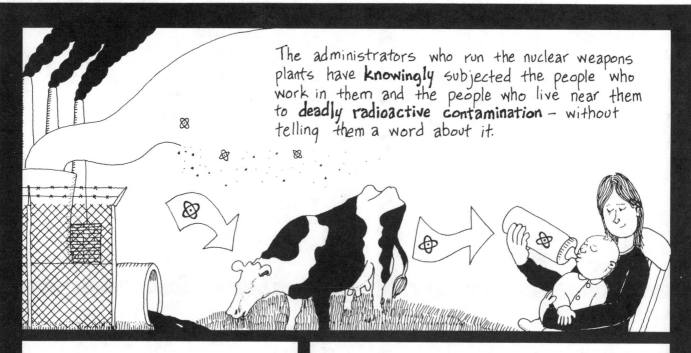

The administrators who run the nuclear weapons plants have **knowingly** subjected the people who work in them and the people who live near them to **deadly radioactive contamination** – without telling them a word about it.

The government now estimates it will take **25,000 workers** at least **30 years** to clean up the mess at these plants – at a cost of **$300 billion** or more.

(133)

And guess who's **paying the bill!**

Beep Beep

What's more, nuclear weapons tests have spread deadly **plutonium** across large tracts of the Southwest and the South Pacific. Many of the 458,000 U.S. soldiers who participated in the atomic testing program are now **dying of cancer**.

(134)

Don't worry, kid. It's perfectly safe. Just wear these goggles!

?

US

U.S. ARMY   PVT. GRUNT

But they're not the only ones. **High cancer rates** plague the general population in the testing areas. One study estimated that previous nuclear testing would eventually cause at least **430,000 people** to die of cancer worldwide.

(135)

And plutonium remains **highly radioactive** for hundreds of thousands of years.

Meanwhile, at military bases around the country they've been **dumping hundreds of thousands of tons of toxic wastes,** including chemical warfare agents, napalm, explosives, PCB's, and heavy metals, creating malignant lagoons and **contaminating the groundwater** of surrounding communities.

There are 11,000 military dump sites that need to be cleaned up. The estimated cost — **$100 to $200 billion.**

(136)

I say let's fence 'em all off and call them **national security sacrifice zones.**

DANGE
KEEP OU
TOXIC W

He's serious — that's what some people are proposing

Another cost of foreign wars is the **retaliation** they bring.

If we weren't always **bombing other people,** we wouldn't have to worry so much about people **bombing us!**

On the eve of the U.S. invasion of Iraq, Homeland Security Secretary Tom Ridge admitted that the war would spur **more terrorist attacks** against the U.S.

(137)

" I think we can anticipate... **more threats** because of a potential invasion. I mean it's **fairly predictable.**"

Tom Ridge, March 2003

In other words, the Bush Administration knew that invading Iraq would bring retaliation, but it decided to go ahead and **place us in greater danger** anyway!

The "War on Terrorism" opened a new chapter in U.S. foreign wars, a chapter that may be marked by an **endless cycle of violence.** Some in Washington seem to **relish the prospect.** Emerging from his secret bunker several weeks after the September 11, 2001 attacks, Dick Cheney predicted that the "War on Terrorism" would go on for a long time. (138)

"It may **never end.** At least not in our lifetime"

CHENEY

Cheney, Oct. 2001

As part of this **endless war**, he declared, we have to be prepared for **ongoing terrorist attacks**.

As a result, Cheney warned, we'll have to get used to **invasive security measures**.

"We're going to have to take steps... that'll become a **permanent** part of our **way of life**"

(140)

Dick Cheney, October 2001

"For the first time in our history we will probably suffer **more casualties** here **at home** than will our troops overseas"

(139)

Dick Cheney, October 2001

Which brings us to **another cost** of militarism — the **loss of our civil liberties**.

We **never said** this war was not going to have **costs!**

As the United States **barricades itself against the world**, we all suffer the inconveniences of increased security measures. But some of these measures are not simply inconvenient — they are **dangerous**.

Grrrr

"Homeland security" has become a slogan for eliminating civil rights protections long deemed inconvenient by the **FBI** and other **police agencies**.

Agencies that often give priority to **suppressing political opponents**

52

You can now be **jailed indefinitely** without trial.

The police and the **FBI** – and even the **CIA** and the **NSA** – can more easily **spy on you,** reading your mail and e-mail, listening in on your phone, and breaking into your home.

Thousands of immigrants have been **called in for questioning** simply because they came from predominantly Muslim countries. (141)

Many have been jailed for long periods on **baseless suspicions**

Nearly everyone in this country pays a high price for militarism. But those among us who have paid the **highest price** are the **millions of soldiers** who have been sent overseas to fight.

More than **100,000 U.S. soldiers and sailors have died** in foreign wars since U.S. troops were sent to Korea in 1950. (142)

Hundreds of thousands more have been wounded, many **disabled for life.** Many Gulf War veterans are suffering the effects of **"Gulf War Syndrome."**

Those who survive continue to be **haunted by the wars** they fought in. Hundreds of thousands of soldiers returned from Vietnam, Iraq and Afghanistan with **post-traumatic stress disorder** caused by memories of the horrors of war. And war veterans suffer from high rates of **depression** and **suicide**. (143)

Hundreds of thousands of military veterans have ended up living on the streets. (144)

And the **killing goes on**, even between wars.

Every year, more than a thousand U.S. soldiers and sailors are killed in **military accidents**. They are burned to death in fires at sea, crushed by tanks, and blown up by practice artillery fire.

BOOM

U.S. NAVY

They break their necks jumping out of planes in high wind and crash in **unsafe helicopters**.

SNAP

?!

(145)

These are all victims of Washington's **addiction to militarism**. And there are more victims...

Every year, hundreds of active-duty soldiers and sailors **commit suicide**.

US ARMY   PVT. JONE

Of course, nobody is **born** with a desire to be **humiliated and treated like a "grunt"**, much less to be killed. So **indoctrination** into the culture of militarism starts early.

Bang! Bang! You're dead!

Television, movies, video games, and toy stores all make **killing** seem not only glorious, but **fun**.

Eat lead, scumface!

Cool!

High school principals lock the doors and hire armed guards, supposedly to protect the kids from **drug dealers, pimps, and other dangerous characters.** But they roll out the red carpet for the **most dangerous characters of all** — the **military recruiters**.

ARMY

NAVY

AIR FORCE

MARINES

The recruiters, who are not quite as honest as used car salesmen, come armed with **slick brochures and glossy promises**.

Just **sign here** and you'll get money for college and we'll train you to be a **nuclear physicist!**

Cool!

U.S.

U.S.

By the time the recruits find out what **military life** is really all about, they're **trapped**.

I said **lick it up** — you got that, **wormhead!**

The ones who end up on the **front lines** are usually kids who can't find a job or pay for college. Almost all of them are from **working-class families,** and a disproportionate number are African Americans, Mexican Americans, Puerto Ricans, Native Americans, and other national minorities. As a result, it's mostly the poor who **die on the battlefield.**

That's why **22% of U.S. casualties** in Vietnam were **Black** soldiers.

Even though Blacks only make up **12%** of the U.S. population.

(146)

The **greatest injustice** is that the people who start the wars are not the ones who fight and die.

My daddy told me I could **serve my country** better by going to **law school!**

For **some people** war means handsome profits and overseas investment opportunities.

STOCK PRICES

DAILY NEWS

IT'S WAR!

U.S. WILL PREVAIL —PRESIDENT

For **others** the price of war is high.

Mission accomplished!

Unfortunately, the costs of wars are **paid** by people who have little to do with starting them!

A veteran who was paralyzed by a bullet in Iraq wrote a letter to George W. Bush and Dick Cheney shortly before he died:

"You sent us to **fight and die** in Iraq after you, Mr. Cheney, dodged the draft in Vietnam, and you, Mr. Bush, went AWOL from your National Guard Unit. You were not willing to risk yourselves for our nation, but you sent hundreds of thousands of young men and women to be **sacrificed in a senseless war** with no more thought than it takes to put out the garbage. I have, like many other disabled veterans, come to realize that our mental and physical wounds are of no interest to you. We were **used**. We were **betrayed**. And we have been **abandoned**. I hope that before your time on earth ends, as mine is now ending, you will find the strength of character to stand before the American public and the world, and in particular the Iraqi people, and **beg forgiveness**."

Tomas Young, 1979-2014

(147)

Chapter 7
Militarism and the Media

So how come every time there's a war, so many people support it?

That's another **good** question

Most Americans are **not very eager** to fight wars halfway around the world.

Here

Uhh... lemme **think** about it

In order to win public support, pro-war politicians have always had to wrap foreign wars up in **red, white and blue** and tell Americans that it's their **patriotic duty** to support them.

?

TIC TIC

Still, it would be hard to convince people without the help of the **news media**, especially the television networks. When it comes to war, the networks discard all **pretenses of objectivity**.

Bomb 'em back! Bomb 'em back! **Waaaay** back!

abc FOX NBC CNN

After the 1991 Gulf War, one of the Bush Administration's top war planners spoke to a group of **prominent journalists** and thanked them for their help.

(148)

" [Television was] our **chief tool** in selling our policy."

Richard Hass, National Security Council, 1991

It sure was. We were treated to live 24-hour war coverage, **sponsored by** Exxon and General Electric and **cleared by** the Pentagon.

Just **how many lives** can these new high-tech weapons **save,** Colonel?

When the Pentagon is **preparing to invade** a foreign country, the news media faithfully repeat the **official justifications** for war and paint monstrous pictures of the **enemy of the hour.**

Reliable sources reported today that _____ eats **babies for dinner.**

Fill in the blank

Lawrence Grossman, who was in charge of **PBS** and **NBC News** for many years, described the role of the press this way:

(149)

"The job of the President is to set the agenda and the job of the press is to **follow the agenda** that the leadership sets."

As a result, you get just about the **same message** no matter what channel you turn to.

Our game plan is right on schedule...

Our game plan is right on schedule...

Our game plan is right on schedule...

Why do all the networks sound the same? Why are they all **consumed by war fever** every time the White House decides to send troops overseas?

Maybe it's got something to do with **who controls them**

The TV networks are owned by some of the largest corporations in the world and members of the boards of directors of these corporations also sit on the boards of **weapons manufacturers** and other companies with **vested interests** around the world.

(150)

Our networks tell you everything you **need to know**

XEROX Honeywell CHRYSLER BOEING Rockwell Automation

In fact, the corporations that control the television industry are fully integrated into the **military-industrial complex**.

For example, let's take a look at the **media empire** of one of America's premier military contractors — **General Electric**

GE has major investments around the world, which it expects the Pentagon to protect. It is also a charter member of the military-industrial complex.

A member in good standing, I might add!

GE is the country's third largest military contractor, raking in billions of dollars every year. It produces parts for every nuclear weapon in the U.S. arsenal, makes jet engines for military aircraft, and creates all kinds of profitable electronic gadgets for the Pentagon. It's also the company that secretly released millions of curies of deadly radiation from the Hanford nuclear weapons facility in Washington state and produced faulty nuclear power plants that dot the U.S. countryside.

"We bring good things to life!"

Top executives at GE have long been aware that in order to keep billions of Pentagon dollars flowing into its coffers it was necessary to build public support for massive military spending. In 1950, President Truman named Charles Wilson, GE's board chairman, to head the Office of Defense Mobilization. In that capacity, Wilson told members of the Newspaper Publishers Association:

(151)

"If the people were not convinced [that the Free World is in mortal danger] it would be impossible for Congress to vote the vast sums now being spent to avert this danger. With the support of public opinion, as marshalled by the press, we are off to a good start. It is our job — yours and mine — to keep our people convinced that the only way to keep disaster away from our shores is to build up America's might."

Charles Wilson, 1950

(Of course, Wilson and his buddies at GE expected to get their hands on a hefty chunk of those vast sums.)

Under Wilson, GE got into the media business itself to promote its **pro-war message**. In 1954, it hired a **floundering actor** named Ronald Reagan to be its **corporate spokesman**. GE furnished Reagan with an all-electric house and gave him his own TV show, which was called **"GE Theater."**

It also furnished Reagan with **"The Speech,"** GE's political message for America, and sent him around the country to deliver it. He continued to deliver variations of "The Speech" throughout his career.

Meanwhile, GE was busy **buying up** TV and radio stations across the country.

Then in 1986, GE bought **its own TV network – NBC**. It had owned the network for 27 years when...

Breaking news – **Comcast** has bought our network from **GE** for $23 billion dollars. But **don't worry** – despite the ownership change you can still trust everything we say.

The huge corporations that own the news media are **hardly unbiased sources** of information. Yet most of the news available to us – about war and peace and everything else – is **filtered through their perspective**. This gives them a powerful influence on public opinion.

Everyone is rallying behind the President

Hmmm...

But their influence is not as complete as they **might hope**.

Chapter 8
Resisting Militarism

In fact, there's been **strong opposition** to foreign military adventures since the Mexican-American and Spanish-American wars of the 19th century. The **anti-war movement** grew especially strong during the war to conquer the Philippines.

"I have seen that we do not intend to free but to **subjugate** the Philippines. And so I am an **anti-imperialist**. I am opposed to having the **eagle put its talons on any other land**... I have a strong aversion to sending our bright boys out there to fight with a **disgraced musket** under a **polluted flag**."

Mark Twain,
Vice President,
Anti-Imperialist League,
1900

Let's go back to Charles Wilson's era, when he and the media were **mobilizing support** for the **Korean War.** At first they were very successful. But despite their impressive efforts, the support **didn't last long**. After the body bags started coming home, the majority of people turned against the war.

I want my son back home! Now.

The government and the media once again did their best to whip up support for the war in Vietnam. But as the **war escalated**, the greatest anti-war movement in U.S. history arose. At first, the opposition was **small but determined**.

BRING OUR MEN HOME

But opposition **grew by leaps and bounds** as people began to learn what was going on in Vietnam. By 1969 there were 750,000 people **marching on Washington,** and millions more marching in cities across the country.

In May 1970, after police and National Guard troops **fired on anti-war demonstrations,** killing four students at Kent State in Ohio and two students at Jackson State in Mississippi, students at 400 universities across the country went on strike — the **first general student strike** in U.S. history. (155)

When police shot and killed three people during the **Chicano Moratorium** against the war in August 1971, a rebellion raged through East Los Angeles for three days. (156)

Resistance to the war took many forms. People **refused to pay war taxes.**

Paycheck

People **burned their draft cards.**

Hell no, we won't go!

63

The most famous **draft resister** was Muhammad Ali.

I won't serve in a **white man's war!**

People **blocked the path of trains** hauling troops and munitions bound for the war.

STOP THE WAR!

STOP THE TRAIN

14,000 people were arrested when they moved to **shut down Washington, D.C.,** for three days in 1971.

It was the largest mass arrest in U.S. history!

(157)

Even more serious for the Pentagon, **discipline was breaking down** among the troops in Vietnam. The soldiers saw no reason to fight, and they wouldn't. By the end of the '60s, a **virtual civil war** simmered between soldiers and officers. A U.S. military expert warned the Pentagon about the state of its army: (158) (159)

"[By] every conceivable indicator, our army that now remains in Vietnam is in a state **approaching collapse**, with individual units avoiding or having **refused combat, murdering their officers** and non-commissioned officers, drug-ridden and dispirited where not **near mutinous.**"

Col. Robert Heinl, U.S.M.C. retired, 1971

FTA

Record numbers of soldiers and sailors **deserted or went AWOL.** Organized resistance was developing among the troops. Hundreds of **underground G.I. newspapers** were springing up at bases around the U.S. and around the world. Contingents of soldiers and sailors were marching at the head of anti-war demonstrations.

Soldiers coming home from Vietnam were telling the country about the **horrors of the war** and they were organizing to stop it. In April 1971, more than a thousand **Vietnam veterans** gathered at the Capitol Building in Washington and **threw back the medals** they had received in the war.

(160)

By the end of the decade, the majority of the people were **against the war.**

The **anti-war movement**, together with the **struggles** waged by African Americans, Latinos, Native Americans, and other oppressed peoples in the U.S., and the women's liberation movement were opening people's eyes to a **whole system of injustice.**

The growing opposition to the war played an important role in convincing the government that it **had to pull out** of Vietnam.

"The **weakest chink in our armor** is American public opinion. Our people won't stand firm in the face of heavy losses, and they can **bring down the government."**

President Lyndon Johnson, 1968

(161)

As a result of the Vietnam War, a broad anti-militarist sentiment developed among the American people, which was derisively called the **"Vietnam Syndrome"** in official circles.

Don't talk about that **dreadful disease!**

Because U.S. leaders knew that Americans would not stand for large numbers of U.S. war casualties, they had to **restrain their military impulse.** They kept on bombing other countries, but for almost two decades they did not send large numbers of U.S. soldiers to fight on foreign soil.

Until 1991...

Then when George H.W. Bush did send hundreds of thousands of U.S. troops to the Persian Gulf, people were **very apprehensive.** The majority did not want to go to war. A powerful anti-war movement grew more quickly than ever before in U.S. history.

Soon the **streets were filled** with demonstrations.

Immediately after the war began, hundreds of thousands of people marched in San Francisco and Washington, D.C.

George the Elder knew he had to finish the war quickly and with few U.S. casualties or the people would **turn against it.** When Iraq chose to withdraw rather than fight and the war ended with a **one-sided slaughter,** Bush was **euphoric.**

" **By God,** we've kicked the **Vietnam Syndrome** once and for all!"

AMERICA IS NO. 1 –AND DON'T YOU FORGET IT!

(162)

After 9-11, George W. Bush set out to test his father's proposition. He promised us a **long and bloody** "War on Terrorism."

(163)

" So long as anybody's terrorizing established governments, there **needs to be a war** "

George W. Bush October 17, 2001

Americans were stunned by the **horror** of the September 11 attacks and Bush's bellicose words resonated among many. But others were **not so easily led.**

Thousands march to protest U.S. war plans for Afghanistan, Washington, D.C., Sept. 2001

Then as Bush was gearing up to invade Iraq, hundreds of thousands of people **took to the streets** across the country. It soon became clear that the **Vietnam Syndrome** was alive and well— a huge part of the population remained profoundly skeptical about **foreign military adventures.**

Many of the country's largest **labor unions** and **church federations** resolved to oppose the war. Over **150 cities,** including New York, Los Angeles, Chicago, Philadelphia, Detroit, San Francisco and Cleveland went on record opposing the war.

"Empty Warheads Found in Washington"
NO WAR IN IRAQ

That **never** happened before— not even in the 1960s!

Regime change begins at home!

67

The whole world was angry. On **February 15** and **16, 2003,** millions of people in the U.S. and over sixty other countries participated in the **largest international protest in history.**

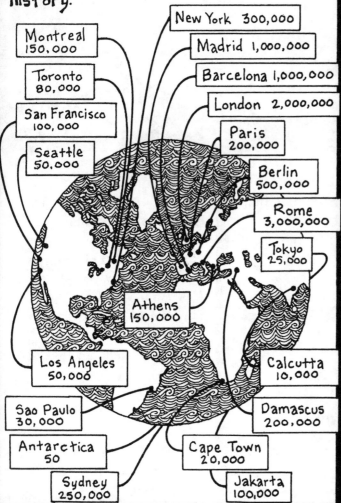

Montreal 150,000

Toronto 80,000

San Francisco 100,000

Seattle 50,000

New York 300,000

Madrid 1,000,000

Barcelona 1,000,000

London 2,000,000

Paris 200,000

Berlin 500,000

Rome 3,000,000

Tokyo 25,000

Athens 150,000

Los Angeles 50,000

Calcutta 10,000

Sao Paulo 30,000

Damascus 200,000

Antarctica 50

Cape Town 20,000

Sydney 250,000

Jakarta 100,000

The great majority of Americans were **not at all eager** to go to war. Most people told pollsters they opposed invading Iraq if Bush could not win U.N. support or if a war would result in large numbers of casualties among U.S. troops or Iraqi civilians. After Bush launched the invasion, however, the **pro-war media blitz** convinced many people that they shouldn't oppose the war because that might endanger U.S. soldiers.

(164)

The media forgot to mention that it was Bush who **put us in danger** in the first place.

And that the best way to get us out of danger is to **get us out of here!**

There were a few pro-war rallies, but not many people showed up.

Turn Baghdad into a **parking lot!**

Operation **I**raqi **L**iberation

68

The war ended up **polarizing** the American population and **isolating** the United States internationally. And the **ugly reality** of the American occupation of Iraq has further alienated people here and around the world.

Don't they know that **God** is on **our** side?

The Next Chapter
Do Something About It!

Here are **a few groups** that are trying to figure that out...

We've only been able to include in this list a small number of the many groups conducting anti-militarist education and organizing anti-war activities in the U.S. Some of the most vibrant organizations are local groups that we were not able to include here. More organizations are listed on Frank Dorrel's website (www.addictedtowar.com). We encourage you to contact groups whose activities are most closely aligned with your own concerns, beliefs, and talents.

American Friends Service Committee
1501 Cherry St., Philadelphia, PA 19102
(215) 241-7000
afscinfo@afsc.org; www.afsc.org

ANSWER Coalition
617 Florida Ave. NW
Washington, D.C. 20001
(202) 265-1948
info@internationalanswer.org
www.answercoalition.org

Center on Conscience & War
1830 Connecticut Avenue, NW
Washington, DC 20009
(202) 483-2220
ccw@centeronconscience.org
www.centeronconscience.org

CODEPINK
666 G Street NE, Washington DC 20002
(202) 248-2093
info@codepink.org
www.codepink4peace.org

Fellowship of Reconciliation
P.O. Box 271, Nyack, NY 10960
(845) 358-4601
info@forusa.org; www.forusa.org

GI Rights Hotline
(877) 447-4487
girights@girightshotline.org
www.girightshotline.org

Global Network Against Weapons & Nuclear Power in Space
P.O. Box 652, Brunswick, ME 04011
(207) 443-9502
globalnet@mindspring.com
www.space4peace.org

International Action Center
147 W. 24th St. 2nd Fl., NY, NY 10011
(212) 633.6646
iacenter@iacenter.org; www.iacenter.org

Iraq Veterans Against the War
P.O. Box 3565, New York, NY 10008
(646) 723-0989
www.ivaw.org

Office of the Americas
(310) 450-1185
ooa@igc.org
www.officeoftheamericas.org

Peace Action
8630 Fenton St., Ste. 524
Silver Spring, MD 20910
(301) 556-4050; (310) 565-0850
info@peace-action.org
www.peace-action.org

The Project on Youth and Non-Military Opportunities
P.O. Box 230157, Encinitas, CA 92023
(760) 634-3604
www.projectyano.org

School of the Americas Watch
5525 Illinois Ave. NW
Washington, DC 20011
(202) 234-3440
info@soaw.org
www.soaw.org

Teaching for Change
(800) 763-9131; (202) 588-7204
info@teachingforchange.org
www.teachingforchange.org

United for Peace and Justice
P.O. Box 607, New York, NY 10108
(212) 868-5545
info.ufpj@gmail.com
www.unitedforpeace.org

Veterans for Peace
216 S. Meramec Ave., St. Louis, MO 63105
(314) 725-6005
vfp@igc.org
www.veteransforpeace.org

Voices for Creative Nonviolence
1249 W. Argyle St. No. 2, Chicago, IL 60640
(773) 878-3815
info@vcnv.org
www.vcnv.org

War Resisters League
339 Lafayette Street, New York, NY 10012
(212) 228-0450
wrl@warresisters.org
www.warresisters.org

Women's International League for Peace and Freedom
11 Arlington St., Boston, MA 02116
(617) 266-0999
wilpf@wilpf.org
www.wilpf.org

World Beyond War
P.O. Box 1484, Charlottesville VA 22902
davidcnswanson@gmail.com
www.worldbeyondwar.org

And for news and views that **you won't hear** on the **corporate news media**, you can listen to...

Democracy Now!
The War and Peace Report

A daily news program hosted by Amy Goodman and Juan Gonzalez. Broadcasting on Pacifica, NPR, community and college radio stations, as well as on PBS, public access and satellite TV, and the internet.
www.democracynow.org

Reference Notes

1   For updated information on the U.S. military budget see the National Priorities Project website (www.national priorites.org). Discretionary spending must be appropriated by Congress every year, as opposed to mandatory budget items such as social security benefits and interest payments on the national debt.

2   Giles cited in Howard Zinn, *A People's History of the United States* (Harper-Collins 1980), 153.

3   Zinn, 125–146; Dee Brown, *Bury My Heart at Wounded Knee: An Indian History of the American West* (Holt, Rinehart and Winston 1971).

4   Black Elk cited in Brown, op. cit., 419.

5   Zinn, op. cit., 147-166.

6   Denby cited in David Healy, *U.S. Expansionism: The Imperialist Urge in the 1890s* (University of Wisconsin Press 1970), 122-123.

7   Platt cited in Healy, op. cit., 173.

8   Roosevelt cited in Zinn, op. cit., 290.

9   Zinn, op. cit., 290-305; Beveridge cited in Zinn, op. cit., 306.

10 Beveridge cited in Healy, op. cit., 174.

11 Beveridge cited in Rubin Westin, *Racism in U.S. Imperialism* (Univ. of South Carolina Press 1972), 46.

12 Zinn, op. cit., 305-313; Michael Parenti, *The Sword and the Dollar* (St. Martins Press 1989), 42-43.

13 Zinn, op. cit., 290-305.

14 On Hawaii see Joseph Gerson, "The Sun Never Sets," in Joseph Gerson, ed., *The Sun Never Sets - Confronting the Network of Foreign U.S. Military Bases* (South End Press 1991), 6, 10; On Panama see T. Harry Williams, et al., *A History of the United States [Since 1865]*, 2nd edition (Alfred Knopf 1965) 372-373.

15 David Cooney, *A Chronology of the U.S. Navy: 1775-1965* (Franklin Watts 1965), 181-257.

16 Catherine Sunshine, *The Caribbean: Struggle, Survival and Sovereignty* (South End Press 1985), 32.

17 George Black, *The Good Neighbor* (Pantheon Books 1988), 31-58; Sunshine, op. cit., 28-34.

18 Taft cited in William Appleman Williams, *Americans in a Changing World* (Harper & Row 1978), 123-124.

19 Newspaper report cited in Westin, op. cit., 226.

20 Sunshine, op. cit., 83.

21 This and subsequent passages are from Smedley Butler, *War Is a Racket* (Round Table Press 1935).

22 Page cited in William Foster, *Outline Political History of the Americas* (International Publishers 1951), 362.

23 Foster, op. cit., 360.

24 CFR/State Department policy statement cited in Lawrence Shoup and William Minter, *Imperial Brain Trust: The Council on Foreign Relations and U.S. Foreign Policy* (Monthly Review Press 1977), 130.

25 CFR memorandum cited in Shoup and Minter, op. cit., 170.

26 *Hiroshima-Nagasaki: A Pictorial Record of the Atomic Destruction* (Hiroshima-Nagasaki Publishing Committee 1978), 17.

27 Truman cited in Paul Boyer, *By the Bombs Early Light: American Thought and Culture at the Dawn of the Atomic Age* (Pantheon 1985).

28 The bombing was also intended to preempt Soviet involvement in the war against Japan. See Zinn, op. cit., 413-415.

29 Welch cited in Victor Perlo, *Militarism and Industry: Arms Profiteering in the Missile Age* (International Publishers 1963), 144.

30 Gerson, op. cit., 12.

31 Korea Int'l War Crimes Tribunal, *Report on U.S. Crimes in Korea: 1945-2001* (Korea Truth Commission Task Force 2001), xi; U.S. Dept. of Defense, *Selected Manpower Statistics, Fiscal Year 1984* (1985), 111.

32 Sunshine, op. cit., 142; Black, op. cit., 118.

33 Noam Chomsky, "Patterns of Intervention," in Joseph Gerson, ed., *The Deadly Connection: Nuclear War and U.S. Intervention* (New Society 1986), 66; Zinn, op. cit., 469; Sean Murphy et al., *No Fire, No Thunder: The Threat of Chemical and Biological Weapons* (Monthly Review Press 1984), 22-24, 64, 78-79; Parenti, op. cit., 44; U.S. Dept. of Defense, op. cit.; Marilyn Young, *The Vietnam Wars: 1945-1990* (Harper-Collins 1991).

34 Robert Fisk, *Pity the Nation: Lebanon at War* (Oxford University Press 1992); Sandra Mackey, *Lebanon: Death of a Nation* (Congdon & Weed 1989).

35 Black, op. cit., 156.

36 Schultz cited in Black, op. cit., 156.

37 Noam Chomsky, *The Culture of Terrorism* (South End Press 1988), 29; *Associated Press*, "Libyan Court Wants Americans Arrested for 1986 Bombing," March 22, 1999.

38 Noam Chomsky, *Fateful Triangle: The United States, Israel & The Palestinians* (South End Press 1999).

39 William Blum, *Killing Hope: U.S. Military and CIA Interventions Since World War II* (Common Courage Press 1995).

40 Jack Nelson-Pallmeyer, *School of Assassins* (Orbis Books 1999).

41 Charles Bergquist, et al., *Violence in Colombia: The Contemporary Crisis in Historical Perspective* (Scholarly Resources 1992); W. M. Leo Grande and K. Sharpe, "A Plan, But No Clear Objective," *Washington Post*, April 1, 2001; Mark Cook, "Colombia, the Politics of Escalation," *Covert Action Quarterly*, Fall/Winter 1999.

42 Peter Wyden, *Bay of Pigs: The Untold Story* (Simon and Schuster 1979).

43 Richard Leonard, *South Africa at War: White Power and the Crisis in Southern Africa* (Lawrence Hill 1983); Richard Bloomfield, ed., *Regional Conflict and U.S. Policy: Angola and Mozambique* (Reference Publications 1988); Alex Vines, *RENAMO: Terrorism and Mozambique* (Indiana University 1991); Joseph Hanlon & James Currey, *Mozambique: Who Calls the Shots?* (Zed 1991).

44 Reagan cited in Black, op. cit., 170.

45 John K. Cooley, *Unholy Wars: Afghanistan, America and International Terrorism* (Pluto Press 2000).

46 Chalmers Johnson, "American Militarism and Blowback," in Carl Boggs, ed., *Masters of War: Militarism and Blowback in the Era of American Empire* (Routledge 2003), 113-115.

47 National Security Council document cited in *New York Times*, Feb. 23, 1991.

48 Doug Ireland, "Press Clips," *Village Voice*, Nov. 13, 1990.

49 Tim Wheeler, "Reagan, Noriega and Citicorp," *People's Daily World*, Feb. 25, 1988.

50 Kenneth Sharpe and Joseph Treaster, "Cocaine Is Again Surging Out of Panama," *New York Times*, Aug. 13, 1991.

51 Tom Wicker, "What Price Panama?," *New York Times*, June 15, 1990; Nathaniel Sheppard, Jr., "Year Later, Panama Still Aches," *Chicago Tribune*, Dec. 16, 1990, 1; Associated Press, "Ex-Senator Says U.S. Massacred Panamanians," *Chicago Tribune*, Nov. 15, 1990.

52 Daniel Yergin, *The Prize: The Epic Quest for Oil, Money, and Power* (Simon and Schuster 1991), 200-202; Michel Moushabeck, "Iraq: Years of Turbulence," P. Bennis and M. Moushabeck, eds., *Beyond the Storm: A Gulf Crisis Reader* (Olive Branch Press 1991), 26-28.

53 State Dept. statement cited in Joseph Gerson, et al., "The U.S. in the Middle East," in Gerson, op. cit., 167.

54 Michael Tanzer, *The Energy Crisis: World Struggle for Power and Wealth* (Monthly Review Press 1974).

55 The Ba'ath Party was soon thrown out of the government, but came back to power in a 1968 coup that was also aided by the CIA (Roger Morris, "A Tyrant 40 Years in the Making," *New York Times*, March 14, 2003; Moushabeck, op. cit., 29-30).

56 Kissinger cited in Hans von Sponek and Denis Halliday, "The Hostage Nation," *The Guardian*, Nov. 29, 2001.

57 Alan Friedman, *Spider's Web: The Secret History of How the White House Illegally Armed Iraq* (Bantam Books 1993); Clyde Farnsworth, "Military Exports to Iraq Under Scrutiny, Congressional Aides Say," *New York Times*, June 24, 1991; Michael Klare, "Behind Desert Storm: The New Military Paradigm," *Technology Review*, May-June 1991, 36; Philip Shenon, "Iraq Links Germs for Weapons to U.S. and France," *New York Times*, March 16, 2003.

58 Christopher Dickey and Evan Thomas, "How Saddam Happened," *Newsweek*, Sept. 23, 2002; Elaine Sciolino, "Iraq Chemical Arms Condemned, But West Once Looked the Other Way," *New York Times*, Feb. 13, 2003.

59 Philip Green "Who Really Shot Down Flight 655?" *The Nation*, Aug. 13-20, 1988, 125-126.

60 Bush cited in Yergin, op. cit., 773.

61 Hitchins, op. cit.; Bush cited in *Newsweek*, Jan. 7, 1991, p.19.

62 Michael Klare, "High Death Weapons of the Gulf War," *The Nation*, June 3, 1991; Malcolm Browne, "Allies Are Said to Choose Napalm for Strikes on Iraqi Fortifications," *New York Times*, Feb. 23, 1991; John Donnelly, "Iraqi cancers offer clues to Gulf War Syndrome: Uranium residue a prime suspect," *Miami Herald*, April 6, 1998.

63 Bush cited in Mitchel Cohen, "'What We Say Goes!' How Bush Senior Sold the Bombing of Iraq," *Counterpunch*, Dec. 28, 2002.

64 Middle East Watch, *Needless Deaths in the Gulf War: Civilian Casualties During the Air Campaign and Violations of the Laws of War* (Human Rights Watch 1991); Mark Fireman, "Eyewitnesses Report Misery, Devastation in the Cities of Iraq," *Seattle Times*, Feb. 5, 1991; George Esper, "500 Die in Bombed Shelter in Baghdad," *Chicago Sun Times*, Feb. 13, 1991; David Evans, "Study: Hyperwar Devastated Iraq," *Chicago Tribune*, May 29, 1991.

65 "War Summary: Closing the Gate," *New York Times*, Feb. 28, 1991; Associated Press, "Army Tanks Buried Iraqi Soldiers Alive," *Greeley Tribune*, Sept. 12, 1991.

66 Bush cited in Robert Borosage, "How Bush kept the guns from turning into butter," *Rolling Stone*, Feb. 21, 1991, 20.

67 Ramsey Clark, *The Fire This Time: U.S. War Crimes in the Gulf* (International Action Center 2002), 64-64, 209; Thomas Nagy, "The Secret Behind the Sanctions: How the U.S. Intentionally Destroyed Iraq's Water Supply," *The Progressive*, Sept. 2001.

68 John Pilger, "Collateral Damage," in Anthony Arnove, ed., *Iraq Under Siege: The Deadly Impact of Sanctions and War* (South End Press 2000), 59-66.

69 Noam Chomsky, *A New Generation Draws the Line: Kosovo, East Timor and the Standards of the West* (Verso 2001), 11.

70 Nick Wood, "U.S. 'Covered Up' for Kosovo Ally," *London Observer*, Sept. 10, 2000; Norman Kempster, "Crisis in Yugoslavia, Rebel Force May Prove to be a Difficult Ally," *Los Angeles Times*, April 1, 1999; Diana Johnstone, "Hawks and Eagles: 'Greater NATO' Flies to the Aid of 'Greater Albania,'" *Covert Action Quarterly*, Spring/Summer, 1999, 6-12.

71 Noam Chomsky, *The New Military Humanism: Lessons from Kosovo* (Common Courage Press 1999).

72 Bin Laden cited in *Wall Street Journal*, Oct. 7, 2001.

73 Bush cited in "The President's Words," *Los Angeles Times*, Sept. 22, 2001.

74 Bosch cited in Alexander Cockburn, "The Tribulations of Joe Doherty," *Wall Street Journal*, reprinted in the *Congressional Record*, Aug. 3, 1990, E2639.

75 Ibid; John Rice, "Man with CIA Links Accused of Plotting to Kill Castro," Associated Press, Nov. 18, 2000; Frances Robles and Glenn Garvin, "Four Held in Plot Against Castro," *Miami Herald*, Nov. 19, 2000; Jill Mullin, "The Burden of a Violent History," *Miami New Times*, April 20, 2000.

76 Joe Conason, "The Bush Pardons," http://archive. salon.com/news/col/cona/2001/02/27/pardons/.

77 Bosch cited in Cockburn, op. cit.

78 Blum, op. cit.

79 Unnamed member of a group of CIA and Special Forces paramilitary operatives cited in Bob Woodward, *Bush at War* (Simon and Schuster 2002), 352.

80 An investigation based on press reports estimated that U.S. bombing killed between 3100 and 3600 Afghan civilians during the first year of the war (Marc Herold, "U.S. bombing and Afghan civilian deaths: The official neglect of unworthy bodies," *International Journal of Urban and Regional Research*, Sept. 2002, 626-634).

81 Carlotta Gall, "Rights Groups Report Abuses by Afghans, Some Backed by U.S.," *New York Times*, July 29, 2003; Amy Waldman, "Afghan Warlords Thrive Beyond Official Reach," *New York Times*, Sept. 24, 2003; Matthieu Aikins, "Afghanistan: The Making of a Narco State," *Rolling Stone*, Dec. 4, 2014.

82 For U.S. military casualties in Afghanistan see http://icasualties.org.

83 Bush cited in Barry Horstman, "We cannot wait for a mushroom cloud," *Cincinnati Post*, Oct. 8, 2002.

84 An Associated Press team surveyed the records of Iraqi hospitals and found unambiguous evidence of at least 3240 war-related civilian deaths (Niko Price, "First Tally Puts Iraqi Civilian Deaths at 3240," *Atlanta Journal-Constitution*, June 10, 2003).

85 Unnamed senior Bush Administration official cited in "Pentagon Expects Long-Term Access to Key Iraq Bases," *New York Times*, April 20, 2003.

86 Powell cited in *The Economist*, April 5, 2003.

87 Edward Wong, "Direct Election of Iraq Assembly Pushed by Cleric," *New York Times*, Jan. 12, 2004; Steven Weisman, "Bush Team Revising Planning for Iraqi Self-Rule," *New York Times*, Jan. 13, 2004. Bremer cited in Booth and Chandrasekaran, "Occupation Forces Halting Elections Throughout Iraq" *Washington Post*, June 28, 2003.

88 See "To the victor go the spoils in Iraq reconstruction," Reuters, April 15, 2003; "The Oil Spoils," *The Nation*, June 16, 2003; Sabrina Tavernise, "U.S. Tells Iraq Oil Ministers Not to Act Without Its OK," *New York Times*, April 30, 2003.

89 Derr cited in Antonia Juhasz, *The Tyranny of Oil* (William Morrow 2008), 337.

90 Juhasz, op. cit., 351-356.

91 Abizaid cited in Juhasz, op. cit., 319.

92 The broader purpose of the U.S. invasion was advanced in *Rebuilding America's Defenses*, published by the Project for a New American Century in Sept. 2000. PNAC members Dick Cheney, Donald Rumsfeld, Paul Wolfowitz, and Richard Perle became key members of the Bush Administration and the paper became a blueprint for the administration's aggressive foreign policy. See: www.newamericancentury.org/RebuildingAmericasDefenses.pdf.

93 Bush cited in "U.S. Attributes Explosion at Iraqi Mosque to Bomb-Making Activity," *New York Times*, July 3, 2003.

94 Swannack cited in Dexter Filkins, "A U.S. General Speeds the Shift in an Iraqi City," *New York Times*, Nov. 18, 2003.

95 The video and a detailed account of the killings put together by Wikileaks can be found at: http://www.collateralmurder.com/. Manning was sentenced to 35 years in prison for releasing the video and other classified materials.

96 Seymour Hersh, "Torture at Abu Ghraib," *New Yorker*, May 10, 2004. Prisoners held by the U.S. military in Afghanistan and Guantanamo, Cuba were treated in similar fashion, indicating systematic practices of torture and abuse approved at the highest levels (Seymour Hersh, "The Gray Zone," *New Yorker*, May 24, 2004).

97 Ashcroft cited in Fox Butterfield, "Mistreatment of Prisoners is Called Routine in U.S." *New York Times*, May 8, 2004. Ashcroft assigned Lane McCotter, who had been forced to resign as director of Utah prisons after a prisoner abuse scandal, to rehabilitate Saddam Hussein's infamous Abu Graib prison, which soon gained renewed notoriety in American hands.

98 Unnamed American soldier quoted in David Rhode, "Search for Guns in Iraq and Surprise Under a Robe," *New York Times*, June 3, 2003.

99 Juhasz, op. cit.; Dexter Filkins, "What We Left Behind: An increasingly authoritarian leader, a return of sectarian violence, and a nation worried for its future," *New Yorker*, April 28, 2014.

100 For up to date estimates of both casualties and financial costs see www.costsofwar.org.

101 Kerry Sheridan, "Iraq Death Toll Reaches 500,000 Since Start Of U.S.-Led Invasion, New Study Says," *The World Post*, Oct. 15, 2013; also see www.costsofwar.org.

102 As of June 2014, the Bureau of Investigative Journalism estimated that US drone strikes had killed between 2977 and 4770 people, of whom 450 to 1089 were civilians and 175-218 were children. http://www.thebureauinvestigates.com/category/projects/drones/drones-graphs/.

103 For more about drone warfare see Medea Benjamin, *Drone Warfare: Killing by Remote Control* (OR Books 2012); Peter Singer, *Wired For War: The Robotics Revolution and Conflict in the 21st Century* (Penguin 2009); Nick Turse and Tom Engelhardt, *Terminator Planet: The First History of Drone Warfare, 2000–2050* (Dispatch Books 2012), and Brian Glyn Williams, Predators: *The CIA's Drone War on Al Qaeda* (Potomac Books 2013).

104 http://www.bga-aeroweb.com/Top-100-Defense-Contractors-2014.html.

105 Hartung, op. cit.

106 Robert Bryce, "The Candidate from Brown & Root," *The Austin*

Chronicle, Aug. 25, 2000.

107 Jane Mayer, "Contract Sport: What did the Vice-President do for Halliburton?" *New Yorker*, Feb. 16, 2004; Angelo Young, "Cheney's Halliburton Made $39.5 Billion on Iraq War," *International Business Times*, March 20, 2013.

108 In 2000, Cheney left Halliburton to run for vice-president but he retained $18 million in stock options and received about $150,000 a year in deferred compensation (Mayer, op. cit.).

109 Jon Wiener, "Hard to Muzzle: The Return of Lynne Cheney," *The Nation*, Oct. 2, 2000.

110 Seymour Hersh, "Lunch with the Chairman: Why was Richard Perle Meeting with Adnan Khashoggi?" *New Yorker*, March 17, 2003, 76-81.

111 See, for instance, a 1996 policy proposal entitled, "A Clean Break: A New Strategy for Securing the Realm" penned by a group of neo-conservative strategists led by Perle for the Netanyahu government in Israel. See: www.israelieconomy.org/strat1.htm.

112 Robert Higgs, ed., *Arms, Politics and the Economy* (Holmes & Meier 1980), Preface, xiii.

113 The 1972 Anti-Ballistic Missile Treaty had outlawed defensive missile systems. See Joshua Cohen, "An Interview with Ted Postol: What's Wrong with Missile Defense," *Boston Review*, Oct./Nov. 2001; David Sanger, "Washington's New Freedom and New Worries in the Post-ABM-Treaty Era," *New York Times*, Dec. 15, 2001.

114 Paul Richter, "Plan for new nukes clears major hurdle," *Los Angeles Times*, May 10, 2003. For updated information on U.S. nuclear weapons policies see the Physicians for Social Responsibility website: www.psr.org.

115 Jeffrey Smith, "U.S. Urged to Cut 50% of A-Arms: Soviet Breakup Is Said to Allow Radical Shift in Strategic Targeting," *Washington Post*, Jan. 6, 1991; Michael Gordon, "U.S. Nuclear Plan Sees New Weapons and New Targets," *New York Times*, March 10, 2002.

116 Judith Miller, "U.S. Seeks Changes in Germ War Pact," *New York Times*, Nov. 1, 2001; William Broad and Judith Miller, "U.S. Recently Produced Anthrax in a Highly Lethal Powder Form," *New York Times*, Dec. 13, 2001.

117 William Broad and Judith Miller, *Germs: Biological Weapons and America's Secret War* (Simon and Schuster 2001); Blum, op. cit.

118 Data are from the Stockholm International Peace Research Institute. http://www.sipri.org/research/armaments/milex/recent-trends.

119 Michael Renner, *National Security: The Economic and Environmental Dimensions* (World Watch Institute 1989), 23.

120 Center for Defense Information, "America's $1 Trillion National Security Budget" March 13, 2014. http://www.pogo.org/our-work/straus-military-reform-project/defense-budget/2014/americas-one-trillion-national-security-budget.html.

121 Timothy Saasta, et al., *America's Third Deficit: Too Little Investment in People and Infrastructure* (Center for Community Change 1991).

122 Jobs With Peace Campaign, *Fact Sheet No. 3* (1990).

123 Saasta, op. cit.; Institute for Policy Studies, *Harvest of Shame: Ten Years of Conservative Misrule* (Institute for Policy Studies 1991), 11; Jane Midgley, *The Women's Budget, 3rd Edition* (Women's International League for Peace and Freedom 1989), 19.

124 A.W. Gaffney, "The Neoliberal Turn in American Health Care," *Jacobin*, April 15, 2014; Venetia Lai and Gwen Driscoll, "Funding shortfall of more than $1.3 billion could push safety-net hospitals to brink," *UCLA News*, June 2, 2014.

125 Institute for Policy Studies, op. cit., 11.

126 Midgley, op. cit., 16; Pam Belluck, "New Wave of the Homeless Floods Cities' Shelters," *New York Times*, Dec. 18, 2001.

127 James Dao, "War Mutes Critics of Costly Carrier Groups," *New York Times*, Nov. 11, 2001. By 2013 the annual operating cost of the latest carrier group had risen to well over $2 billion. See Henry Hendrix, "At What Cost a Carrier?" *Disruptive Defense Papers*, Center for a New American Security, March 2013, 5.

128 Prenatal care costs $625 per mother: U.S. Congress, *Background Material and Data on Programs within the Jurisdiction of the Committee on Ways and Means* (1990).

129 The Head Start program costs $2,600 per student annually: U.S. Congress, op. cit.

130 Private clinics charge about $3,000 per year for intensive outpatient drug or alcohol treatment: Author survey, 1992.

131 Citizens Budget Campaign, *It's Our Budget, It's Our Future*.

132 The cost of the first of at least three new aircraft carriers will be about $13 billion (Hendrix, op. cit.).

133 Keith Schneider, "Military Has New Strategic Goal in Cleanup of Vast Toxic Waste," *New York Times*, Aug. 15, 1991; Matthew Wald, "U.S. Sharply Increases Cost Estimates for Cleaning Up Weapons Plants," *New York Times*, Sept. 6, 1991; H. Jack Geiger, "Generations of Poisons and Lies," *New York Times*, Aug. 5, 1990; INFACT, *Bringing GE to Light* (New Society Publishers 1990), 117-121.

134 Greg Baisden and S. Destefano, "Pool of Tears," *Real War Stories, No. 2* (Eclipse 1991), 1-3.

135 Matthew Wald, "Study Says U.S. Chose Riskier Atomic Test Site," *New York Times*, May 17, 1991. The cited study predicted that 430,000 people would die by the end of the 20th century.

136 Schneider, op. cit.

137 Ridge cited in Philip Shenon, "Ridge Warns That Iraq War Could Raise Terrorist Threat," *New York Times*, March 4, 2003.

138 Cheney cited in Bob Woodward, "CIA Told to do 'Whatever Necessary' to Kill bin Laden," *Washington Post*, Oct. 21, 2001.

139 Cheney cited in David Sanger, "Taking on Another War, Against Mixed Messages," *New York Times*, Sept. 4, 2001.

140 Cheney cited in *Washington Post*, Oct. 21, 2001.

141 For updated information on post-9-11 restrictions on civil liberties see the American Civil Liberties Union's website: www.aclu.org/safeandfree.

142 www.militaryfactory.com/american_war_deaths.asp.

143 David Wood, "Iraq, Afghanistan War Veterans Struggle with Combat Trauma," *The World Post*, July 4, 2012.

144 The U.S. government estimated that 150,000 to 250,000 Vietnam veterans are homeless on any given night (Jason Deparle, "Aid for Homeless Focuses on Veterans," *New York Times*, Nov. 11, 1991).

145 U.S. Dept. of Defense, *Worldwide U.S. Active-Duty Personnel* Casualties (1987), 5.

146 Parenti, op. cit., 79.

147 See the full text of Tomas Young's letter at: www.truthdig.com/dig/item/the_last_letter_20130318.

148 Hass cited in Walter Goodman, "How Bad Is War? Depends on the Images," *New York Times*, Nov. 5, 1991.

149 Grossman cited in Allan Nairn, "When Casualties Don't Count," *The Progressive*, May 1991, 19.

150 For corporate boards on which board members of major media corporations sit, see the Fairness and Accuracy in Reporting website: http://fair.org/interlocking-directorates/.

151 Wilson cited in INFACT, op. cit., 97.

152 INFACT, op. cit., 11, 17, 28, 47-49, 107-110, 118.

153 Benjamin Compaine, et al., *Who Owns the Media?* (Knowledge Industry 1979), 80, 84, 97. Comcast completed the purchase of GE's NBC stake in 2013 (http://en.wikipedia.org/wiki/NBCUniversal).

154 Twain cited in Philip Foner, *Mark Twain: Social Critic* (International Publishers 1958), 260.

155 Zinn, op. cit., 481.

156 Chicano Communications Center, *450 Years of Chicano History* (Albuquerque 1976), 160-163.

157 Zinn, op. cit., 477.

158 David Cortright, *Soldiers In Revolt: The American Military Today* (Doubleday 1975), 5-8; Zinn, op. cit., 476.

159 Heinl cited in Thomas Boettcher, *Vietnam: The Valor and the Sorrow* (Crown 1985), 399.

160 Cortright, op. cit., 1-32, 51-136; Zinn, op. cit., 486.

161 Johnson cited in Richard Barnet, *The Rocket's Red Glare: When America Goes to War* (Simon and Schuster 1990), 346.

162 Bush cited in *Newsweek*, March 11, 1991, 30.

163 Bush cited in "Bush Foresees a War Longer Than Two Years," *International Herald Tribune*, Oct. 18, 2001.

164 See, for instance, Maura Reynolds, "Most unconvinced on Iraq war," *Los Angeles Times*, Dec. 17, 2002.